SenseAble Travel

Travel Tips for Families Living with Sensory Processing Disorder - 2nd Edition

By Jennifer Logan

Published by OT World Pty Ltd
contact@otworld.com.au

2nd Edition: ISBN-13: 978-0-6483705-0-5

1st Edition: ISBN-13: 978-1496043030

Dear Reader,

Please note; all tips are based on my personal travel experience with my family and my experience working with children. They do not constitute any form of advice or a formal recommendation, or replace a therapist's recommendations.

No responsibility or liability is taken by the author or publisher for any injury, loss, illness, accident, legal, social or financial loss or damage incurred by reading or following tips contained or implied in this book, downloadable materials or social media associated with this book. Web links to external sites are provided for information purposes only.

The author and publisher take no responsibility or liability for the content at the link. No affiliate links are included in this book. The links, not affiliated with the author or publisher, are correct at the time of publication, however over time may expire. If you are unable to reach the desired web link, please use your search engine to find the information you are seeking.

Table of Contents

Also by Jennifer Logan

"Walk With Me: An interactive children's storybook."
Available in English, Arabic, French, Simplified Chinese,
Italian and Spanish.

Preface

Life is too short to put off your dreams.

This book was written out of my desire to help families with children who have special needs to be able to travel; whether for the sheer joy of travel and adventure, to access medical services, to visit family, or even just to be able to go to the shops.

As an adult who has grown up with sensory processing disorder (SPD), and now being an occupational therapist working with children and young adults with SPD, I have long wanted to write this book. I wanted to help empower families, to help families connect with each other, have shared adventures, reduce their stress when visiting relatives or friends, and enjoy their holiday together. I can't promise that you will get along with your relatives any better though, and of course, no trip is ever without its little ups and downs. I hope that reading this book you will feel more prepared, that you can have fun and enjoy your time.

Sensory processing and sensory modulation issues affect many people. Autistic children and adults have been able to share many of their different sensory experiences giving us an insight into their world although it can be difficult to comprehend these challenges when your sensory processing is typical.

Sensory processing disorder can range from seeking extra sensory input to being unable to tolerate sensations. It may affect one sense or multiple sensory systems. Experiencing the world through a different sensory lens can be difficult, particularly when you are not able to communicate what is happening. This experience can be isolating and stressful for the child, particularly when the adults in their life label the results of this uncertain sensory world as misbehavior.

Many of the tips in this book will be helpful, especially for children on the spectrum who often have challenges with sensory experiences. SPD also often affects people diagnosed with dyspraxia.

I was one of those undiagnosed, clumsy children who chewed on their shirt and hair, felt like a buttoned up shirt or tie was strangling me, and was always covered in bruises from walking into something or falling off something. I learnt to ride my bike at 12 and write my name at 8.

Another group of children that may have undiagnosed sensory issues are children with behavioural challenges. Some of these children have undiagnosed sensory processing challenge. A child often frustrated, stressed, anxious, having tantrums that may actually be meltdowns, refusing to try new things that cannot otherwise be explained may fall into this category.

I hope the tips in this book are helpful for all of these precious children; that it reduces the burden of the sensory challenges in the multitude of activities involved in travel, so they an enjoy the wonderful outing or holiday with their family and not be overwhelmed as much by the noise, new sights, new smells, tastes, and textures a new environment entails.

While writing this book I often thought of my mother who always described holidays as harder work than being at home. I'm sure she was right, with three kids, one of whom was an escape artist, even a night out visiting a family friend could end up in an area-wide hunt for my younger sister.

My sister was born with Down syndrome, and growing up she was virtually uncontainable. She could climb almost any fence and find any key. We raced desperately to teach her how to swim because she could quickly scale our pool fence. Fortunately, she quickly became an excellent swimmer and we put a secure lock on the back door so that we could keep her away from the pool fence that she could climb in seconds.

The stories contained in this book are based on my experiences. I have frequently travelled within Australia; I was very fortunate to have spent time working as a mystery shopper with an airline, resulting in multiple free domestic flights. Living internationally as an expat for almost 8 years, travel was just a part of daily life. If I wanted to see my family, it was a minimum 15-hour plane ride with an active toddler in tow.

Growing up our family spent time travelling around Australia, I can remember sitting in the back of dad's Holden waiting for him to finish tuning a piano, a job that takes a minimum of 3 hours. This was his way of paying for our holidays, as he would drive around the countryside from one piano tuning job to another, to pay for the cost of the petrol and accommodation during our trip. We spent a lot of time in the car. Mum always had plenty of snacks, books, and colouring activities for us and she would knit and do crosswords; of course, this was before iPads, e-books, and other electronic devices.

We went on bushwalks, went canoeing, swimming, horse riding, visited museums, parks, and even went on steam trains. We had lots of fun memories even when things didn't quite go as planned. Such as the time my parents went grocery shopping, and left my brother and me to go trout fishing on a lovely warm day, wearing t-shirts and shorts. While shopping my parents looked out the window and discovered it was snowing! They then had to race back to rescue us from the sudden turn of the weather.

When I finished school, I was bitten by the "travel bug". I had a wonderful time travelling around Australia with my family every school vacation. With interest I watched the travel shows on television, dreaming about one day going to these exotic destinations, having adventures, and coming home to tell the tales.

When I reached university I had my first tentative overseas trip and suffered terribly from homesickness despite being surrounded by friends. I vowed to a close friend that I would never travel overseas again.

Since then I have travelled throughout Asia, lived in rural NSW and lived as a long-term expat in Singapore and Dubai.

I have literally run through the Sydney International Airport, Bangkok International Airport and Singapore International Airport (in heels!). I have missed flights in the Gold Coast; been grounded by fog in Cairns of all places; been delayed in Ho Chi Minh City by hurricanes and left without drinking water for a day; miscalculated the wet season in Vietnam; had food poisoning in Cambodia, ending up in a Vietnamese hospital; and had an unforgettable time in between.

I loved my time in China, Singapore, Thailand, Cambodia, Vietnam, Malaysia, Indonesia, New Zealand, Nigeria, the United Arab Emirates, and of course Australia, my home. I have a very long list of other destinations that I'm planning to visit.

I enjoyed travelling to Dreamworld™ with my sister. We sat through fifteen rides around the Wiggles World ride in a row and had the ride's theme song stuck in my head for over a month …and it's in my head now as I write this.

While living in Sydney I worked in community services as an occupational therapist, and in that time I came to know many dear families. The stress and strain of the situations so frequently led to parents becoming separated or divorced. It was then a superhuman struggle for many who became single parents, many of whom had multiple children to care for in addition to their child with special needs.

Financial strain, social isolation, and emotional distress are factors contributing to family breakdown for many families who have children with special needs. I will never forget one family who told me that they had not been able to eat out, watch a live sports game or even visit a relative for more than five years due to their son's severe behavioural issues. They told me one of the first things they enjoyed doing as a family after initiating occupational therapy services was to go to a local fast food restaurant to enjoy a burger! Life should not be this restricted. Providing access to varied experiences in a supported loving way is necessary to prepare our children for life, even the long haul flights many parents with young children dread are possible.

Families and children with sensory processing difficulties and behavioural challenges can learn how to manage challenging environments and find strategies to enable the child to feel safe despite the sensory triggers that they may face when there is a change in routine or environment.

The tips in this book are provided simply as a starting point to help you think of what will work for your family, your child, and your destination.

I hope the information provided will help equip you and prepare you for a fabulous trip whether you're going to your local park, a theme park, on a weekend away, or an international adventure.

You are the expert on your child. The ideas in this book can help you plan your trip, problem solve around potential challenges, and come up with some new ideas to help your whole family enjoy the trip.

I have included links to resources in this book to provide ideas and information as a starting point in your search for what matches your family's needs and desires. All links to sites are current at the time of publication, and no affiliate links have been included.

If you would like to talk to other families travelling with children who have special needs you can join our Facebook group Senseable Travel:

https://www.facebook.com/groups/senseabletravel/

This group aims to help families enjoy their journey. You are invited to share your stories, photos, tips, and insights.

On our Facebook page, we post links to accessible travel venues, sensory friendly events, and fun children's activities that can be helpful on a long trip. To see regular updates and ideas like our page:

http://www.facebook.com/senseabletravel

Introduction: Why Travel?

Travelling as a family provides the opportunity to have unique experiences and create new memories. New cultures, new languages, and new foods are all part of travel. Even if you are travelling domestically, areas within a country can vary greatly, with different accents, different subcultures, and different climates often being found within the same nation.

The educational opportunities for children when travelling are endless. The chance to have real-life, hands-on involvement in new activities and create lifelong memories for children is priceless.

Shared activities help to strengthen ties within the family unit and extended family. So many people have family scattered around the world. Having the simple joy of being able to travel to see grandparents, family, and friends can help strengthen these relationships and can enable your children to have the joy of experiencing their cultural heritage.

Apart from travelling for the experience or to see family and friends, you may be required to travel for work, study or medical reasons.

My younger sister has Down syndrome; she achieved one of her dearest wishes to drive a car, while at a theme park on a holiday. It was a fully secured, safe driving range where the vehicle followed a predetermined track. This experience gave her more joy than any gift I could have ever purchased for her, and she has enjoyed watching the videos and seeing the photos of herself driving many times.

Typically, while travelling to a new area you have the opportunity to be more physically active, and to try many novel activities that might not be considered at home. Activities such as walking on bush tracks, canoeing, swimming, boating, and sports games can inspire the whole family to explore new activities that could then be pursued at home.

Travel will push you to solve problems and be creative, building stronger relationships. It will help you to exercise your mental muscles to develop a thick skin for setbacks and focus on the wonders out there in the world.

Changing environments can lead to new opportunities to develop language skills. By allowing families to slow down, see new things and have new experiences. Seeing things up in person can help develop concepts beyond what you can see on the television or in a book bringing in smells, sounds and visual images into the child's learning experience.

Depending on where you have chosen to travel it can be a welcome relief from the sensory overload often found in cityscapes for those with sensory sensitivities. If you are from the city and your child has sound sensitivity a trip to the countryside or camping in the bush could provide much needed mental break from the background noise you didn't even know they could hear.

The process of preparing for travel, accessing the transport, meeting the challenges of a new environment, new people, new routine can be a fantastic opportunity to prepare your child for the challenges they will face everyday in their lives as an adult. The coping strategies you teach them now can help them face these changes as an adult.

Growing up in Sydney there have been days when the city has ground to a halt due to breakdowns in the public transport system. Causing mass anxiety and distress for workers and families all over the city.

This may sound like a simple problem solving situation however there are a myriad of questions we have to ask ourselves when our plans are unable to go ahead.

There are a range of strategies that we can use to determine the best option for us to take. However if you are facing sensory processing difficulties and are already feeling overwhelmed this type of challenge can be almost unbearable, will likely cause anxiety, and may even cause a person to shut down.

You can systematically teach your child how to manage this type of situation and it will help prepare them for the inevitable travel disruptions they will face in their lives.

Before you leave for your destination:

- What alternative travel arrangements can you make?
- How can you access the timetables?
- Do you have an app where you can book an UBER (or similar company)?
- Do you have local taxi numbers saved in your phone in case you cannot access WIFI or data while you are travelling internationally?

- If none of these options are available what will you do in the mean time while you wait for the transportation to be restored?
- Is there a safe place to wait?
- Do I have access to water or a snack?
- Am I able to locate a safe bathroom if I have a long time to wait?
- Do I have appropriate clothes for the weather so I can be comfortable?
- Can you have a meal while you wait and adjust your travel plans accordingly?
- Will you need to notify other people?

- What will you do if this causes you to miss a flight or other connection?

When this type of disruption does occur in your daily life, traffic delays, car breakdowns, bus strikes or train cancellations you can model emotional regulation strategies such as deep calm breathing, positive self-talk and systematic problem solving. Children are so often expected to behave to a higher standard than adults in the same situation expect of themselves.

By showing your child systematically ahead of time how they can calmly, problem solve their way through disruptions and challenges such as a bus strike in a city (that may also be in a foreign county) you are equipping them for life for such occurrences.

Chapter 1: Tips on how to Prepare for a Trip

An essential component to any trip is preparation. There are so many things to consider. This is even more so for those travelling with children. If you then have a child with special needs, there is so much more you have to be prepared for.

Research is easy with the internet which puts fantastic travel guides, up-to-date maps, blogs, and even restaurant menus right at our fingertips. This can be time consuming but it is well worth spending the time to ensure you have accurate information and are able to plan accordingly.

Research tips:

- Search online for travel guides. Blue Planet and Lonely Planet are two well-known guides providing detailed information specific to countries and major cities; being sure you are using reliable resource for your research is essential so you don't end up being scammed by a fake hotel or travel site.

- If you are booking a hotel or flight I have always found using their website to book directly with them has given me the best prices in comparison to third party websites. Additionally when booking through third party websites you are typically subjected to additional cancellation processes and fees.

- Visit the website of specific sites you would like to visit; theme parks, public beaches, museums and national parks typically have websites that provide detailed information, maps, and printable images (which you can use to create your own travel story books to help prepare your child for the trip);

- The local government website for an area usually has great information about attractions and events available in their local area;

- Search YouTube for quality videos about the area you are planning to visit. View first to ensure quality and relevance, and then you can show your children the video to give them a visual presentation of the site you are planning to visit. This is a great option for children who are visual learners and for those who need to understand where they are going and what you will be doing before they can feel comfortable in a new area.

- Join groups on Facebook or other online social groups that provide support to families with children who have special needs. You will be able to share stories, gain insights and travel tips. You may like to join pages or groups related to the area you are visiting. For example, Time Out Magazine, has pages dedicated to their magazine locations all around the world with dedicated segments for kids activities;

- Use Google Maps to view the area where you plan to stay from a satellite view. You can check for proximity to water (especially if your child absconds), or train lines (especially if your child is sensitive to noise). Google Maps street view can allow you to "virtually" walk along streets and check if there are any points of interest or concern near to where you plan to stay.

You need to have a clear understanding of your child and acknowledge their needs. This process can be challenging. It can be hard to identify what your child may find essential, particularly if your child has sensory processing difficulties. As most people are so used to their home environment, they take it for granted. Often it is not until you are trying to fall asleep in a new environment that all the new noises or even smells become apparent. For the sensory sensitive person they are aware of it, all the time.

A child with sensory processing challenges is typically unable to tell you what their sensory experience is like. They may not realise your experience of the world is different from theirs. When they are old enough to understand their experience differs they still may not be able to identify specifically how their world differs and why.

You can only make outside observations. Think about their preferred clothing style, fabrics, food textures, shampoos, soaps, toothpaste, and even different types of room lighting, are there any movements or sounds they may avoid or crave. All of these experiences can have an impact on their sense of well-being.

With the knowledge of your child's needs and preferences, you can work to meet these as closely as possible across a variety of environments. This may mean bringing along devices, such as headphones, weighted toys, and preferred clothes, and checking you are able to access their preferred foods.

Your dream may be an international trip to Walt Disney World but before you go booking your international flights, you need to practice.

Practise with day trips using a small budget. You can start at the most basic steps. For example, if you are planning to go to the beach for a day:

1. Start by checking your child's reaction to some basic features of the beach;
2. Show them videos of the beach;
3. Let them play with sand in a sandpit, and seashells if you can access them;

4. Add water to the sand as they can tolerate it to mimic the sand near the waters edge at the beach;
5. Go to a local pool or splash park to experience the larger body of water;
6. Talk to them about how sand and water feel;
7. Play a CD with sounds of the ocean.

These are small tastes of the sensory input at the beach. Observe, does your child enjoy the sensations or are they overwhelming? This process helps you know how to prepare for your trip. Introduce one aspect of sensory input at a time.

Day Trip Ideas:

- Local beaches
- Parks
- The zoo
- The aquarium
- Local shopping centres
- Restaurants
- Museums
- Movie theatres
- Public transport - a local bus, train, or even a ferry
- Children's indoor play centres
- Bowling alley
- Rock climbing centres
- Ice skating
- Roller skating

All of these activities share sensory features of what you will experience during a holiday. These day trips are a fun way to practise managing these types of environments while you are close to home, where you know the location and have support at hand. You may find you have some wonderful parks and activities for your family in your city that you have not yet discovered. You will learn what you need to pack for your child and how to cope with crowds. You will have a clearer idea of what your child can and can't cope with and for how long. For example, you may find after the noise of a train trip your child needs a quiet space to recover for 20 minutes before they can adjust to the next activity. Knowing this allows you to build the extra time into your schedule. Your family will develop the ability to adapt to these situations and you will have some wonderful family experiences. You can use these activities to take photos and videos to create stories to review for your future trips.

When your day trips are going well, you know what to pack, and your children and yourselves are coping with the demands of the activities, then go ahead and plan a weekend away. Find a great location you would love to explore and spend a night away. Again, you are not investing too much time or money into the trip so if things don't work out as you had planned you do not need to feel too disappointed. You may need to practise this stage multiple times before planning more extensive trips, as a night away from home can be very challenging for children.

There are a number of tools you can prepare such as:

- Develop a sensory toolkit.
- You can update communication systems with required words and symbols for the trip;
- For a child who signs, you can teach them the key signs they may need in the new environment;
- You can create social stories that will help to prepare them for this sudden change in environment, schedule, and demands.

Contacting local support groups for families with special needs children that are in the area you are planning to travel to can be an invaluable resource. They will be able to provide answers to questions that are tailored to that particular area, for example, which pizza parlor provides gluten free pizzas?

One of the best ways I found to get to the heart of a place that you are planning to travel to, is to talk with friends who have travelled there before. They will be able to give you rich stories with details that you will not gain from online research.

Some of my own travel stories include how a shopping centre had four disabled parking spaces but no accessible bathroom, or how a popular restaurant had a beautiful "accessible" bathroom conveniently located for wheelchair users - up one step.

If your child finds it difficult to sleep in new environments, you may want to trial noise cancelling machines, gentle music or ambient sounds CDs designed to aid in sleep, well in advance. Your holiday isn't the time to trial new tools or equipment. Anything you are packing for your child to use should be familiar to your child. You should know how it helps your child and when your child needs it.

Pack comfortable clothing and shoes. I can almost guarantee you will end up walking further than you had planned. Don't do it in high heels.
Public transport providers around the world typically provide discounted or free transportation passes for people who have a disability, and in some countries carers also receive discounted travel passes. If you research the area before your trip, you may be able to access these discounts.

Most importantly, despite all the preparation and planning don't expect your trip to be hassle free. You can expect challenges. If you take the time to anticipate what challenges you might face based on your knowledge of your child, you can take steps to help minimise the distress to your child and family.

Learning to meditate or develop your own strategy to help yourself maintain a calm manner during stress will help you to enjoy your trips even if there are meltdowns, tantrums, missed connections or lost bags or toys.

Ultimately any time you spend preparing yourself and your children will lead to happier travels. Each trip is a learning experience. So don't worry if your first weekend away ends in tears. You know what you can do for the next time. Each time you will become more proficient at handling the inherent challenges travelling entails.

While it is great to have a schedule for your trip, while planning your trip do be careful to build in rest time and don't over schedule yourself.

Purchase good travel insurance and be aware of any exclusions. It is very easy to forget while you're out enjoying your trip but frequently activities like riding a motorcycle or horse-riding are excluded and can result in costly hospital bills if you are injured.

Be aware of local conditions at all times. It is easy to get caught up in a local protest, or even a festival that could lead to missed flights, extra costs and stress.

I miscalculated the monsoon season when visiting Vietnam one year and we enjoyed their torrential rain and knee high flooding with a sense of humor. Fortunately we were still able to do many of the activities we had planned however I learnt the lesson the hard way - if you are finding fantastic holiday deals it is worth checking the seasonal weather to see if there is a good reason for the discounts.

Chapter 2: What should I Pack?

What you should pack is going to vary based on multiple factors.

Where are you travelling? You will need to consider the weather, the culture and the activities you can access.

What is the purpose of your travel? You need to bring along equipment and clothing for the specific events you are planning to do as a family.

I recommend you use this list to create headings for your own list. If you do it on a computer once, then you will be able to print off your quick travel-packing list with adjustments based on your destination. Here's a quick checklist of things to consider:

- Medications;
- Medical kit;
- First aid kit;
- Doctor letters and prescriptions – if you're travelling interstate or internationally I strongly recommend you carry doctor's reports explaining diagnosed conditions and current prescriptions. Some over-the-counter medications are illegal in some countries; for example, painkillers containing a small amount of codeine are illegal in United Arab Emirates and Greece;
- A copy of all important documents when travelling overseas;
- Camera;
- List of emergency phone numbers as these do vary from country to country;
- Embassy phone number;
- Travel insurance information and contact numbers;
- Sensory tool kit (See Chapter 35);
- Favourite toys;

- Favourite clothes – children who have sensory sensitivity or difficulty adjusting to change will prefer to have access to their favourite clothes;
- Foods compatible with dietary restrictions;
- Snack foods your children enjoy;
- Communication devices;
- Charging cables;
- Power adaptor for different countries power plugs;
- Extra batteries;
- Mobility devices and batteries;
- Wet wipes;
- Toilet paper;
- Sunblock;
- Swimming clothes;
- Sleeping aids;
- Earplugs or noise cancelling devices;
- Music players/MP3s/DVD players/handheld gaming devices;
- Safety devices;
- Games for indoors and outdoors;
- Toiletries;
- Cooler bags or esky;
- Plastic bags for wet clothes and other emergencies;
- Ziplock bags – these are so handy to have for packing snacks and storing toiletries to prevent leaking in your suitcase. They are also helpful for sorting small objects, are easily labelled, and can be used to freeze water to create disposable ice packs for cooler bags;
- Nappies – if required. Your child may have been toilet trained for an extended period and then experience a regression when placed in a new, unfamiliar, and potentially stressful environment. Having nappies, particularly for night sleeping, can help reduce anxiety for your child and distress for parents concerned about nighttime wetting in a new environment. Consider your child's personality and

toilet training history to determine if reintroducing night-time nappies may result in a setback in their toileting. You may prefer to carry waterproof liners and additional bedding as a backup if you have concerns your child may experience a regression in toileting skills during a trip.

You may also want to include the following after consulting with your paediatrician, and conduct a trial before your vacation:

- Aromatherapy kit*;
- Rescue Remedy*;
- Melatonin* for jet lag;
- Vitamins* and other nutritional supplements*;
- Mild sedatives*;
- Anti-nausea treatments*
- Homeopathic remedy kit*;

* Discussion with your paediatrician is essential.

Taking these medications may cause side effects that could derail your travel plans. Trial the medications with your paediatrician's supervision while safely at home to ensure you are not trying a new medication while in an airplane or isolated area without medical assistance.

Chapter 3: How can I Help Prepare my Child for the Trip?

If your child is using alternative communication systems, it is essential that you introduce additional cards, photos, or signs that your child will need during your trip. If you are using electronic devices ensure these are uploaded to your device.

You need to provide your child with a means of communicating for the duration of your trip. Please discuss with your speech and language therapist. If you do not have access to a speech therapist at this time, there are some general tips you can implement.

Check you have a way to communicate all of the usual basics – food, water, bathroom, and clothing such as jumpers, hats, and shoes.
Identify which images your child uses most frequently and create an extra copy. Laminate and place these on a key ring. A key ring can be attached to you or your child's pant loop or backpack strap for easy, quick access with important images for visual communication. This will be very helpful when you are constantly on the go and don't have a spare hand to carry a book or device with you. This may serve as a backup should you misplace your communication book. A key ring of the day's schedule can also be created quickly.

Make sure you have included images for all toys and sensory tools being packed.

Include: feelings happy, scared, tired, hungry, thirsty. If you do not already have them, include weather related cards, images or signs, such as hot and cold.

Be sure your child can communicate if they feel sick and where – tummy or head, by including PECS images, sick (head), sick (tummy).

It can be helpful to include a card for "oh no – change of plan" or "oh no it's not working" or similar.

Take time to talk to your child about the trip. One of the best things you can do to help your child prepare for change is to develop a storybook about your trip. In this you can describe the event and the environment that you are visiting.

Talking about an upcoming journey can help prepare your child for a change in language, culture, and weather. If you are travelling internationally, you will be in a beautiful new environment; new sights, sounds, smells, tastes, and even time differences can be extremely challenging when you are travelling with children. If your child has difficulty adapting to small changes in their routine this can be a major obstacle to travel. Practising adapting to change and using your anxiety management strategies in a familiar environment before a change occurs will be beneficial.

A new environment means new expectations and new rules. You can go through all of the expectations such as waiting in line for rides or not touching items in a museum. Explain to your child what to expect, how they should act, how others will act, and what will happen if things don't go to plan.

We will discuss writing stories for your children in more depth later in this book. They are such a valuable resource, particularly in how tailored they are to your family and your situation. Including actual photos of the place or your child can increase their interest and engagement in the story and their ability to relate the experience to themselves.

You can make photo albums with photos from your previous trips and talk about what worked well. What did your child enjoy most? What did you and your child learn?

Place the trip on a calendar that your child can see, and talk about the upcoming trip in the weeks leading up to you leaving.

Working together with your child to create a scrapbook about the journey ahead can be exciting for them. Let them cut and paste images you find, have a countdown. Have a visual packing list and talk to them about what you are taking, what it will be like where you are going, how you will get there, and who will be with you.

Establish and review the rules for your trip. For example:

At the airport:

1. I hold hands with mum when she asks me to.
2. I walk inside the airport.
3. I listen to mum and dad

At the hotel:

1. I do not open the hotel door.
2. I ask when I want to go on the verandah.
3. I listen to mum and dad.

You can check your public library, or browse online for videos showing the place you will be visiting. Look for videos that show people travelling on the modes of transport that you will be using and going to places that you are going, to let your child see how things work and how enjoyable travel can be. Avoid any video that intends to create anxiety. The purpose is to share with your child the joy of exploring the world and help prepare them for the new environment, things and people they will see.

If there are special clothes that your child is required to wear while on your trip, I recommend that you practise wearing these clothes and problem solve around any potential tactile sensitivity issues, such as a swimming costume, cold weather gear or wet weather gear. For example, a child with tactile sensitivity may find plastic raincoats to be extremely challenging to wear. You might experiment with different types of raincoats as there are different styles of fabrics available. You might experiment with wearing long sleeves under the raincoat to prevent it touching their skin directly, or you may find an umbrella is the most suitable solution for your child at this time.

Remember, if you are going to try using any medication for travel sickness or for sleeping I recommend that you consult closely with your medical practitioner regarding the trial and use of these medications or supplements before you travel to a new environment, where you may find yourself without support should you experience any side effects or reactions.

Develop and practise using your sensory toolkit in advance to ensure that everything included provides positive sensory support to your child. For example, noise-reducing headphones can be extremely helpful for children with sound sensitivity; however they can take some time to get used to the feeling of wearing headphones.

Practise using sleep aids such as white noise machines to help your child sleep before you travel as these aids can take some time to adjust to.

The Gro-Blind is a portable blind developed to be easily placed on and removed from windows of different sizes and shapes. These help minimise excess light in your room; this can assist your child to sleep longer.

If you plan to provide a nightlight to your child so that they can manoeuvre safely in the dark in your new environment, I recommend that you trial this in advance to ensure that it does not disrupt your child's usual sleeping routine.

Travelling to Asia, Africa or the Middle East? You might encounter a squat toilet or a bidet. WikiHow has simple descriptions of how to use both with simple line drawn images. I recommend that you review how to use these as you may find that they are the only option available. Toilets labelled as accessible bathrooms will usually have a toilet that can be sat on and more space if assistance is needed. It is common to find toilets without seats, without toilet paper or running water. If you are travelling to an area that uses different styles of toilets do provide support to your children in advance. Discuss what the bathroom might be like before you arrive by showing them simple images and talking to them about the different things they will see in the new country.

Commodes and water hoses are commonly used in Asian and Middle Eastern countries. You will want to actively supervise children as it is very easy to end up drenched if you are inexperienced using these devices.

While visiting a hotel in Indonesia, all three girls I was travelling with ended up soaked when trying to work out the commode system, which unfortunately was set to a very high pressure. They had an embarrassing walk through a five-star hotel from the restroom back through the packed restaurant, having become yet another soaking wet victim of the hotel's complicated commode toilet.

Squat toilets, commodes, and water hoses can be quite intimidating if you have never used them before, but with a little bit of practise you can see it is quite easy. My tip for using a squat toilet when wearing pants:

1. Make sure your pockets are empty;
2. Pull up then pull down – meaning first pull up your pant legs to your knees then pull the waistband down from your waist.
This way you will avoid splashing your pant legs, and you won't get your pant legs on the wet floor. You will

appreciate this tip when you are standing on that floor. You don't want that stuff on your pant legs!

You can role play and discuss various scenarios you expect for your trip, for example, having to wait in a queue for a ride at a theme park.

If your child has difficulty with transitions, which is common for children who have autism and sensory processing disorder, you can work on transitioning between tasks as a general skill in advance of your trip. Tools that people find helpful to prepare for moving on to the next activity include: stop light systems which help to prepare you for change; timers; visual schedules; or reward systems can also be beneficial. An occupational therapist can help you determine which approach can help your family.

In our family, we have found providing approximately 5 minutes warning that it is time to go or time to stop an activity eases the children's ability to move from an activity to the next, even when they are engaged in a preferred activity. However, forgetting to give notice can result in a tantrum.

Chapter 4: Child Safety Tips

Trying to prepare for a trip without packing the majority of the household contents is a challenge!

The main safety issues facing families staying in hotels and holiday rental accommodation are similar to the safety issues faced within the family home. Burns, drowning, absconding, and falling are common concerns. Whatever safety steps you are taking within the family home will need to be taken while on holidays. Below are some tips to help address those concerns.

If you are travelling to a cold area, check in advance if the accommodation will have exposed heaters or fireplaces. If so take along your own small, safe heater.

Take along cupboard locks and other safety devices you are using at home.

You may wish to take along toilet lid locks if your child has a history of flushing items or using the toilet inappropriately. I know a nanny who had her passport, mobile phone, and keys flushed by her young charge.

If your child has reduced mobility, it may be helpful to have portable handrails or a plastic bath hose that can be attached to the spout on either the bathtub or the sink if you are unable to access the bath safely.

Travel will reveal a noticeable difference in the self-care routines of people from country to country. When I lived in an apartment in Singapore, the shower was over the toilet. Imagine the bathroom layout – as you stood up from the toilet the handheld shower hose was mounted on the wall directly in front of you, there was no space to stand or move around. You could literally sit on the toilet while having a shower. Your child may refuse to bathe in these conditions. I recommend you ask about the bathroom before booking the accommodation if you are concerned about your child's ability to be flexible in situations like this.

Does your child escape? If so investing in personal safety devices could be helpful. GPS tracking devices or child locators are now widely available. GPS tracking devices can be as simple as a watch or placed on a belt. A similar product is a personal locator which is a waterproof device. This device will sound an alert when the child wanders more than a pre-set distance from the base. Practise having your child wear any devices to ensure they are comfortable and are not likely to be removed. Brands differ in both price and effectiveness, so it is recommended to read the product description and customer reviews closely.

At the very least ensure your child has a wristband with your contact details on it. Your child could wear an ID bracelet with their name and your contact number and medical information such as allergies.

It may take some time for your child to get used to the feeling of wearing a band, particularly if your child has tactile sensitivity. You can see examples of these products at:

http://www.mypreciouschild.com

If your child tends to wander at night there are mattress alarm systems that detect unassisted bed exits, such as:

http://www.alimed.com/over-mattress-alarm-system.html

If you are walking out in a crowd, are near a dangerous area such as standing on a train platform or bushwalking near cliffs, you may want to use a walking harness as a backup (with the loop around your wrist), in case your child drops your hand.

There are simple to use mobile phone devices that can be set up with emergency contacts. An older child who can operate the device can use it to reach out for help. Security officials would also be able to call "mum" or "dad" and know that they have the contact details for you at hand, even if they are not able to recall names or phone numbers.

Teach your child to swim, as soon as possible. As a minimum safety precaution, they need to be able to cope with falling in a body of water while fully clothed, float on their back or paddle to the side and yell for help. This skill can save your child's life.

If your child escapes, or is known to wander, consider informing the staff in advance so that if they see your child out on their own they will immediately alert you.

The FBI Child ID app is available free from the FBI and can be downloaded directly from the iTunes store. This app is designed to keep pictures and critical information in a clear format that can be provided to security and police immediately. This would be particularly useful should you go through the distressing experience of losing your child, you will have the information you need to give to the authorities.

http://www.fbi.gov/news/stories/2011/august/child_0805 11

Labelling all belongings and clothing, with both the name and contact number of the family can help reunite parents with children, particularly when they cannot communicate. Other options discussed above will be beneficial, such as ID bracelets and GPS tracking systems.

Of course, never leave your children unattended at any time. News reports of abducted travellers occur from time to time. I recommend seriously reconsidering plans to travel to areas known for child abduction unless it is necessary and you are in a position to provide personal security for your family.

If your child is non-verbal or becomes non-verbal when under serve stress (such as being separated from a parent) or you are travelling in a country that speaks a language your child does I recommend attaching PECS cards on a key ring attached to their backpack if they are wearing one or attached to a loop on their pants so they can request basic assistance. These only need to be small cards, even as small as 1 inch will be adequate. The child's name, your name with a passport photo and contact number should be included on this. The name of the hotel you are staying in, written in the local language is also helpful if you are travelling internationally.

Chapter 5: My Child has Unexpected Tantrums. How can I Deal with this if it Happens in a Public Place while Travelling?

Unexpected tantrums can be a major obstacle for families wanting to access activities within their community. Meltdowns occur when a child is overwhelmed and unable to communicate or cope with the experience they are undergoing. For children who have sensory processing issues, a brief shopping trip can involve a wide array of overwhelming sensations. What may look like a tantrum may actually be a meltdown.

Being able to identify when a child is having a meltdown, which often appears as an unexpected tantrum can help families reduce the frequency and duration of the meltdown.

Identifying known triggers, empowering the child with strategies to help manage their emotions, working to reduce sensitivities by providing calming sensory input, and removing or avoiding sensory triggers, rather than punishing the "behaviour" is required to assist the child's access to their family and community activities.

Families with children who have special needs often have a tendency to reduce the number of activities they are involved in due to a combination of factors. The increased difficulty of getting around, having so many commitments with other children, and child therapy sessions take up so much time and money from the family budget. Additional equipment and extensive planning required to engage in activities may be barriers to their participation.

Often families simply don't have the energy or finances to go out regularly, which can sometimes result in more challenging behaviours during outings as it is an unfamiliar experience for the child.

If you are planning to travel, then practise aspects of the future experiences close to home when you have help available, and getting into the car and going home is an option. Being in a crowded environment can be a major challenge for people with sensory sensitivities. Lighting, crowds with people brushing up against you, noise, and complex visual patterns are common in shopping centres, markets, and outdoor community events.

Make a storybook, emphasise the expected behaviour, for example, "I hold mummy's hand when we walk in the shop" with a picture of your child holding your hand.
What do you want them to do while waiting in line?
What do you want them to do while waiting for food at a restaurant or in a food court?

Tell them what you expect them to do, be reasonable, and give them the tools they need. For example, "while I am waiting for my food I will play with my toy" with a picture of your child at the table playing with the toy you provide.

Do be fair. It is unreasonable to expect a child to quietly wait in line for extended periods of time; it is unfair to expect them to be out all day at a mall during sales times.

We have a family rule; don't go into a toy store with a child if you aren't ready to buy them a toy. The same rule applies to the food court – don't go to the food court if you aren't ready to buy your child food.

Plan ahead and problem solve around anticipated issues. Practise while you are close to home, and adjust your plan to meet unexpected issues. Your child will learn how to manage in these environments with support over time. Do keep in mind that it may always be a challenge for them, and they will need your encouragement and support, and possibly some relaxation time or a reward after the experience.

It cannot be emphasised enough – learn your child's signals. Each child has individual signals that indicate they are becoming overwhelmed.

It is important to know the difference between a sensory meltdown and a behavioural issue. A sensory meltdown is where you child's body is trying to block out overwhelming sensory input to prevent sensory overload. They are trying to protect themselves from a perceived threat, and they will have little control over their actions once they reach this stage.

A meltdown is not the time to discipline or verbally coax your child. You need to remove as much sensory input as possible. Go to a quiet area if possible, provide deep pressure (proprioception), or give them a hug. Talk in a calm, soothing voice. Let them know you are with them and support them.

Sensory overload can cause sensory shutdown. A child that is becoming overwhelmed will often become fussy, irritable or have a tantrum. This behaviour has a function; it reduces the sensory input and clearly signals to others that they have had enough.

Failing to respond to these signals will likely lead to sensory shutdown. During sensory shutdown your child may appear drowsy or disoriented. You may be unable to rouse them or get their attention. Additionally, they may lose some of their functional abilities; the child may feel nauseated and vomit.

Respond to your child at the very first signs of sensory overload by reducing sensory inputs as soon as possible. Noise reducing headphones (reduce sound), sunglasses or a hat (reduce light), firm hugs or massage (reduce light touch and provide proprioceptive input). This strategy is a natural parenting response to young children, we hug, rock, and shush (this provides white noise) our babies and young children to help them calm down when they are distressed.

Identify a "safe place" when you arrive at a new venue, where you can take your child if they begin to have difficulties. Often, this might have to be your vehicle or an accessible bathroom, however, an empty café or a play area in a store during quiet store hours may be options if you respond to your child's signals early, before they begin to experience a sensory meltdown.

It is recommended you don't travel alone with your child if they are prone to tantrums or meltdowns. Of course, that isn't always possible; however, travelling with a family member or friend who is familiar to your child will greatly alleviate the challenges of travelling, such as, being able to juggle luggage, children, papers, accessing bathrooms, and so on. If this isn't an option, consider if you can hire a support worker to accompany you on your trip.

Request help from your local university; in particular, university students studying education, occupational therapy, speech and language therapy, or similar would respond to such an advertisement. Use your wisdom in hiring anyone working with your child, and complete working with children checks and any other legal requirements as per your local laws.

When you are out on a trip and your child has a meltdown, if it is a safety issue, then it isn't the time to worry about ideal practices. Do what it takes to keep your child safe. That might mean bundling them up and going straight to the car. Don't worry about managing your child's behaviour or what anyone thinks, keep your child safe. Include what happens when they are feeling overwhelmed in their storybook that you have created for them, work out what causes it and find a strategy to get around it.

We are not talking about a temper tantrum here. Your child hasn't been "naughty" so don't treat it as such. They are doing the best they can to keep themselves safe in an overwhelming, sensory world. You are their best ally; there will be another trip and another day to go out. Treat each trip as a practice run and a learning opportunity for your child and yourself. You are learning what works well for them.

If your child is having a temper tantrum, which is a behaviour based response to demands or the environment, they can sometimes respond to discipline or reinforcement at early stages. Avoiding known triggers is advisable.

> My sister would often have a temper tantrum while at the store if she saw DVDs. If she saw one she wanted she would yell, grab, and demand to buy it – even when she had the identical DVD already at home. Avoiding strolling through this area of the store would avoid a very predictable outcome.

Maintain a calm state. Dr. Becky Bailey, in her book "Conscious Discipline", encourages adults to discipline themselves first then the child. If you are unable to control yourself you will not be able to assist your child.

Be consistent with your response. If you say, "no, no, no, no … okay, yes" then you have taught your child that to get something they want they just need to ask repeatedly and they will eventually get it. Stick to your decision and your child will learn that "no" means "no".

If your child throws themselves on the ground crying and they get what they want – you have taught them, that behavior is how they get what they want. The only time I would suggest giving in to a child is when there is a physical safety risk. Being consistent is essential.

All children need consistency in their lives. We all know the scenario where children ask one parent and get a "no" then run and ask the other who says "yes". This behaviour encourages your child to manipulate and persist in asking when you have said no.

Remember what is cute now won't necessarily be cute when your child is 15, or 25, or 55. Children need to learn how they are expected to behave, now is the time to develop their ability to hear, "no" when necessary. A 5-year-old on the ground screaming because they can't get a new toy is hard, but failing to deal with the behaviour as soon as possible can lead to lifelong behavioural issues.

Be reasonable and be consistent. If you need assistance managing your child's behaviour you can seek help from an occupational therapist or behaviour analyst.

Strategies for Managing Tantrums

If you know your child is having a tantrum rather than a sensory-based meltdown you may find the following tips helpful.

Avoid known triggers when possible.

Avoid doing chores in public, such as shopping or going to the bank if you and your child are hungry, over tired or already agitated. Children are much more likely to have a tantrum over a small issue if they are already hungry, tired, or have had an otherwise challenging day.

The most important step is to remain calm yourself. Becoming frustrated, angry, or embarrassed when dealing with a tantrum in public or at home can lead to taking actions that you wouldn't usually do and may later lead to regret. You're not going to get anywhere with your child if both of you are screaming at each other. Take a deep breath and keep control over your emotions.

Clearly and simply indicate to your child that the tantrum behaviour is not acceptable. This may be simply saying "no" with head shaking and hand showing the stop signal.

The earlier you are able to intervene in the tantrum the higher the chance you will have of being able to diffuse the situation. Once your child is in a full-blown tantrum you will likely have to wait it out; children are typically not able to regain control of themselves once they are in this state.

Stay close by until the tantrum is over. Don't try to stop your child or reason with your child when they are out of control. Never use the threat of abandonment.

If your child is having a public tantrum, focus on keeping them safe. You may have to carry them to a safe area such as your car in the car park. Once you are in a quieter place, try to ignore the tantrum until it stops. If your child continues to scream, place him securely in his car seat and drive home, if you can do so safely. Calming stating, "I am waiting for you to calm down" is far more effective at diffusing a situation in comparison to threatening to leave, or otherwise punishing the child.

Holding your child in a firm hug and slowly rocking can sometimes calm a child who is having a tantrum.

When you talk to them, keep your message short and clear. Do not use abusive language to your child during a tantrum; your focus should be diffusing the situation.

If your child is engaging in aggressive behaviours during the tantrum, ensure your child is safe and that they are not able to hurt themselves or others. This may require you to move them to a safe area, or remove items around them.

If your child is having a tantrum to get something, do not give it to them during the tantrum as you will be teaching them how to get what they want in the future, and will strongly reinforce these behaviours. If you want to give the item to your child when they have calmed down, they need to "earn it". That may simply be asking nicely for the item, or what you determine is fair, such as finishing a task before "earning" the item.

If your child is having a tantrum to escape a task, do not allow them to escape the predetermined task. For instance, a child who was requested to pack away their toys – following the tantrum they should be calmly returned to the initially requested task.

Check:

1. Did your child understand what was requested of them?
2. Was the task fair?
3. Was the task within their ability to complete?
4. Do they need step-by-step instructions?
5. Do they need additional support to complete the task?

You may need to modify the task to ensure your child can complete it successfully. Then follow through to ensure the task is completed. Allowing your child to escape from non-preferred activities, such as packing away, doing homework, or doing age/developmentally appropriate chores, by having a tantrum clearly teaches them how to get out of non-preferred tasks.

Remember after a tantrum, your child may need to be held and reassured, as they may be tired and scared of their lack of control or strong reaction.

Praise your child for calming down. Be specific in your praise "Good boy", "good girl", "good work" is not specific enough. Reinforce and praise the actions you want to see more of. This might look like, "you took deep breaths, you held my hand tight, you calmed down".

Does your child have an appropriate way of expressing frustration or anger? Is your child able to negotiate tasks and rewards? For instance, if they want to play outside are they able to express that to you either verbally or non-verbally so that you can use it as a reinforcer for completing required tasks? For example, put your toy's away and then we will go and play outside.

After a tantrum, comfort your child without giving into her or his demands. Tell your child that he or she was out of control and needed time to calm down.

As an adult it is essential we model appropriate strategies to our children. I often see adults punishing their children for the very same behaviour the adult engages in when they feel frustrated.

Teach and model other ways to handle anger and frustration. Teach your child different ways to deal with negative emotions. This may help reduce the number of temper tantrums a child has. Offer simple suggestions to help a child learn self-control. For example, encourage your child to use words to express feelings; or establish a safe, comfortable place in the home where your child can go to calm down.

Ensure that you notice and praise your child's good behaviour. If your child is using tantrum behaviour to get attention find positive ways to lavish your attention on your child, and reinforce positive behaviours you see. Verbal praise should clearly state what they did well. "Good boy" or "good girl" shows them you are happy with them.

Make eye contact with your child if they are comfortable with this, get down to their level and use clear language to describe what they have achieved. For example, "you listened to me", "look you coloured inside the lines", "you sat still during the story, great sitting still", "you picked up all your blocks and put them in the box", and so on. This

45

shows your child what they did well and helps them to repeat their success because they understand what they have achieved.

Use this strategy to greatly increase the degree and specificity of your praise on your child while you reduce your response to undesirable behaviours such as tantrums.

Ensure you have calm, quiet responses to tantrums, and in comparison, enthusiastic, specific, attentive responses to desired behaviours. This can take practice; tantrums can be embarrassing and stressful for the parent. Dr. Becky Bailey's website https://consciousdiscipline.com/ has outstanding resources for parents and caregivers, where she encourages adults to discipline themselves first then respond to the child.

Chapter 6: What if Security Staff or Police Become Involved?

In the unlikely event that you or your child becomes involved with security or law enforcement staff, please keep in mind just like all individuals, the understanding of law enforcement officers of the special needs community is going to vary dramatically from country to country and from individual to individual.

We would all hope that officers would be understanding and compassionate. To assist them I recommend the following while travelling:

- Carry doctor's letters clearly explaining the diagnosis and how this is evidenced. Particularly highlight any heart, hearing, vision, or cognitive impairments in clear simple language;
- Carry copies of clearly written prescriptions for any medications you are carrying that you or your child requires;
- Carry disability and carers cards;
- Carry identification cards for your child (or passport copies);
- Scan and store copies of these in your smartphone as PDF files and in your email accounts, so you can access them anywhere in the world. If you don't have a smartphone, take a photograph of the documents;
- If you are travelling to a non-English speaking country translate these documents into the local language before you travel. You may consider carrying a card in the local language stating what your child's disability is and what that means in practical terms.

Do not travel internationally if you do not have travel insurance. Most travel insurance companies include a fund for legal aid and may contribute toward repatriation costs.

The consulate will provide assistance to their citizens under certain criteria if you find yourself facing an emergency.

Australian's can register their travel plans with the Department of Foreign Affairs and Trade by following the link found on: https://dfat.gov.au/Travel/Pages/travel.aspx

Chapter 7: Preparing for Air Travel – The Airport

If you are fortunate to live near Philadelphia International Airport in the USA, they offer the Airport Autism Access program, open to people who have special needs. Wings for Autism is now running events allowing people who have autism, along with their families, to rehearse the entire process of air travel in various airports throughout the USA. If you live close to the airport you can visit, watch people check in, watch planes take off, take a photo of your child at the airport, and even board the plane. They are aiming to run their programs at domestic airlines across the USA.

You can visit **www.thearc.org/wingsforautism** for more information.

If you are planning an international flight, it would be helpful to take a short domestic flight before you try your longer international flight. Use the trip to problem solve for future travels, take plenty of photos for your story books, and videos for you to use to remind them of their trip, and when preparing for your next trips.

You can watch clips on YouTube depicting the stages of checking in, going through airport security, customs, boarding, the flight, disembarking, baggage claim, customs, and your arrival.

You can print maps and pictures of your local airport from their website if your child enjoys viewing these.

Include the airport in your child's storybook about their upcoming journey. If you are concerned about how your child will cope during the flight, you can create a storybook for your child about their upcoming flight.

When booking your flights advise the airline of your child's needs in advance. Carefully consider where you are booking your seats on the flight; proximity to bathrooms can mean disruptions throughout the night on long haul flights.

Advise airport staff your child has a hidden disability, let them know if your child has difficulty understanding instructions. Let the staff know if your child may become upset during the screening process, and what they may do during an outburst. At no point should you leave your child unattended, including if they need to be screened privately.

If you have concerns regarding your child's ability to process through security screenings, please contact your local airport and review the Transportation Security Administration (TSA) website **www.tsa.gov** for specific information on requirements and alternative options they can offer.

Before you leave the house for the airport, ensure your child is not carrying anything on themselves or in their carry-on luggage that might set off alarms.

While travelling with my parents, my sister who is an adult diagnosed with Down syndrome, was carrying a toy with a metallic part. When it set off alarms, she refused to part with the toy. It took quite some time to retrieve the toy and calm everyone down. You can imagine the scene, she was unhappy, we were unhappy, and then there were the security guards…

Airport security guards need to do their job. A behavioural issue during check in and security screening will cause them to go on high alert. This may lead them to adopt threatening behaviour towards a child or young adult who will not comply with instructions, particularly if they start shouting and fighting with you. If your child has a hidden disability, their attitude and actions will likely be harsher as their first assumption will not be that your child has a learning disability. The staff will do what they see as necessary to provide security. Discussing your concerns and requirements with the airline and airport prior to travel will help eliminate any unnecessary concerns.

A set of keys, a few coins in their pocket, or a mechanical or electronic toy can be enough to set off detectors or result in you having to remove the item from your child, whether they are willing or not. Also, watch for liquids and electronics in your carry-on luggage. We now completely and easily avoid this situation by doing a quick check before getting into the car to go to the airport.

Avoid having to unpack and repack at security screenings when travelling, especially when you are travelling with children. Be fastidious about ensuring carry-on luggage complies with airline restrictions. Additionally, think of what you and your child are wearing, large belt buckles are notorious for setting off alarms.

After arriving late to the airport terminal I was further delayed when my travelling companion had to remove their jacket, watch, shoes, and belt before successfully being able to clear the security checkpoint at the airport. In their highly anxious state, my companion absentmindedly threw their jacket through the metal detectors for me to hold. This caused airport security to spring into action. Fortunately, by standing still and following instructions the situation was quickly diffused. This type of situation can be avoided by dressing simply: Think leggings or track pants and a simple shirt. Forget fashion and go for comfort. It will make the flight more relaxing and will help you as you enter the airport.

If you are flying with an infant, you may find using an infant sling or carrier to be helpful. It can take a while for your child to get used to being in a carrier. If you are travelling with an infant and they are used to being in a sling, or a baby carrier, do not forget to bring it along, it will be very handy, giving you free hands for other children, your documents, and luggage.

When flying with children, using backpacks as carry-on luggage instead of suitcases will free your hands up to hold children's hands, push trolleys, and to handle your travel documents. Backpacks for your children have the added benefit of providing calming proprioception, while carrying their toys, entertainment for the flight, and a change of clothes. Ensure the bag is not overloaded; no more than 10 percent of your child's body weight is a good guide.

When he was a baby, I regularly put my son in a sling when going for walks, shopping, and even just for around the house. This became invaluable when going through the airport terminal while travelling alone with my infant, as the airline I was travelling with did not allow prams past the security checkpoint. I still had to juggle my son, our travel documents, and our carry-on luggage. Having the sling made it so much easier. I had to remove him from the sling when passing through customs and the security screening. Aside from this, for the remaining 2 hours waiting for the flight, I had somewhere comfortable for him to sleep while I was walking around the terminal, standing, or sitting to read before I boarded the plane.

Chapter 8: Preparing for the Flight

What you can carry onto the plane is quite restricted, so you will need to make careful choices about what you bring on as carry-on and what you choose to stow.

Try to use your time at the airport to move around as much as possible before a long flight. While you are walking give your child a backpack to carry or a trolley with some bags in it to provide weighted resistance for them to push (if they are available in the terminal).

Before boarding allow your child to access their sensory tools that you have brought along, such as chewies, sound therapy devices, and stretchy toys, or anything that you have found from experience to be calming for your child.

Having an iPad or electronic device prepared with your child's favourite programs and games can be very helpful. Providing less access to this in the weeks coming up to the trip can help increase the desirability of the device, which may help your child maintain their interest in the device for longer.

Have some affordable toys prepared as gifts or rewards during the trip. These can be wrapped individually as a little surprise for your child to help keep them entertained.

Bring along some treats your child can enjoy, within their dietary needs. To increase the desirability of the treat it can be helpful to minimise access to these for a few weeks before your journey. Having something to suck on during take off and landing can help children clear their ears.

Ensure you have meals for your child if they have special diets, as airlines often not cater well for allergies. If you are flying to countries such as Australia or New Zealand, you will find strict regulations regarding the foods and other items that can be brought into the country. Remember to declare any food you bring with you off the plane to avoid fines.

You can use a blanket to create a "time out" space both in the airport and on the plane.
Walk around the plane when allowed, as there are often areas where you can have a small amount of space that will allow you to complete some simple exercises with your child.

Dr. Becky Bailey's book, "Love Rituals", has a lovely collection of rhymes and hand games that can be played with children in a small space. You may find this helps to distract and entertain children within the constraints of an airline seat.

Use your sensory tool kit filled with tools you know are helpful and enjoyable for your child.

Make sure your child has had plenty of movement before the flight where there ability to move around will be constrained for an extended time period. It can be easy to forget during the rush to get out of the house.

If your child is a sensory seeker jumping on a mini trampoline, hanging from a chin up bar, even running on the spot or any of their favourite movement exercises before they leave the house can help them cope with having to sit for so long. For children who avoid excess movements going for a walk, even walking on the spot, hanging from a chin up bar, gently bouncing on a physio ball can be helpful and these activities can be completed in the house while you are doing your final preparations for the trip.

Chapter 9: Preparing for International Travel

Before you leave check your phone has international roaming. International SIM cards are available which can help reduce the cost of calls from overseas. Smartphone apps such as Whatsapp, Skype, and Facetime can reduce call costs when used over Wi-Fi. International data roaming is typically extremely expensive. Turning the data off on your phone and limiting apps access to your data bundle can save thousands of dollars in unexpected phone expenses.

Public libraries, cafes, shopping centres, and hotels are good sources of free or cheap Wi-Fi access.

You may want to prepare a card that states in the local language your food requirements. For example, if you are a vegetarian and want to request no meat having this written in the local language with the English pronunciation for yourself can be helpful.

If you intend to drive you may want to apply for an international driver's licence, and check the local road rules and insurance arrangements in advance.

If you are not planning to drive research taxi numbers and store in your phone, so you do not find yourself out without being able to reach a taxi.

If you or your child has physical limitations, check the phone numbers for an accessible taxi in advance, and remember that you may need to book well in advance (24 hours or more).

I also recommend storing the phone numbers for emergency services in your phone as these do vary from country to country.

When leaving the hotel ensure you collect a hotel business card to show taxi drivers, particularly if you do not speak the local language.
Remember, do your research, including travel insurance, and medications you can carry into the country and limits applied to these medications.

Visit both your paediatrician and travel doctor to discuss immunisations and medications, and obtain documentation for all medications including over the counter ones.
Prepare all documentation, scan and email to yourself, store printed copies in an accessible part of your luggage, separate to the originals.

Packing your bag carefully in advance when flying will make your boarding much easier. Have a separate bag for items that must be removed for security screening such as, liquids, toiletries, and electronic devices. This will help you to avoid the stress of digging through bags looking for these items while you are at the security screening checkpoint. Planning ahead will make your time at security checkpoints as smooth and easy as possible.

Fly direct to avoid short stopovers, which can result in additional delays and layovers in a third foreign country. Stopovers may require additional visas and will double the landings and take offs (if air pressure changes are a challenge for your child this may well be a significant factor in your decision). However, if you are planning to stay for a few days, a stopover can be a nice way to break up an extended flight and see another country.

During the flight, it can be more comfortable to wear slip on shoes. Have noise reducing headphones and sound therapy programs available.

Keep your sensory tools, games, electronic devices, and any special food for your child accessible for your flight by placing them in their bag.

Chapter 10: How can I Juggle Everything?

While in transit you will have luggage, documents, your handbag, and most importantly your children to keep track of in a busy, new environment. It is easy to become flustered with the stress of the airport environment combined with the fatigue often caused by long flights.

Remember your child comes first; do not lose hand or eye contact with them at any time while transiting. Even your documents can be replaced with some effort.

If flying, I recommend you use a trolley to manage your luggage, and check-in as much as possible. Carry only the essential items through the airport, which will still be quite substantial, especially if you have children on special diets or requiring sensory items while on a plane.

Remember you can ask airport staff for assistance, and if you aren't able to take a pram through customs, you can often access a small trolley from the duty-free store.

Use an oversized stroller for children who struggle to walk long distances.

Attach yourself to your child. You may want to use a child harness with the loop around your wrist, in case your child drops your hand to run. A boogie board or surfboard cord can also be used to link yourself with your child when walking in higher-risk areas, such as bushwalking along cliff tops, areas with water, in airports, train stations, or busy markets. Hold your child's hand and use it as a backup.

Ensure your child is wearing ID and use your storybook or discussions to help them to know what to do if you become separated; this is essential for all of your children as even older children (and adults) can wander off unexpectedly.

You may find travellers pouches can be helpful to keep track of documents and money, especially if some of your clothing does not have pockets, and this can help protect you from pickpockets.

Follow the usual travel tips, such as don't leave your wallet or other important materials in your back pocket as it makes you a target for pickpockets, and email scanned copies of all important documents to yourself and carry printed copies separate to your original documents. Always look back and check an area as you leave to ensure you are not leaving things (or people) behind.

Ensure you have travel insurance, check what they will and won't cover, and itemise any valuables you are carrying before travelling. It is common for travel insurance policies to exclude activities such as accidents occurring during winter ski sports, driving a motorcycle, and scuba diving beyond certain depths.

Some airports offer additional assistance for a fee. The fee may be waived if you have a diagnosed disability. For example, Marhaba services available in Dubai airport have a range of services; families can benefit from having a staff member greet them at the airport with a pram, assist with carry-on bags and luggage, or assist with immigration procedures. For additional fees, luggage can be delivered to your accommodation.

For further information and to make bookings see:

https://www.marhabaservices.com

Chapter 11: Tips for Jet Lag

Exercise and sunlight on arrival at your destination for at least one hour can help reset your internal clock; this will help both you and your child adjust to your new time zone.

You may find your children do not adjust to the new time zone. You may choose to allow them to remain in your home time zone and simply eat and sleep at their usual time. This may work for you if the time zone differs by a few hours. However, if your child is not adjusting to larger time differences, you may want to try medications.

Some people have found melatonin and clonidine (by prescription) to be helpful for jet lag. Again, I suggest you trial any medications before departure with your pediatrician's supervision.

Having experienced jet lag with toddlers, I recommend going through a similar process as you do with a newborn when you first teach them to sleep through the night.

- During the day give them lots of attention, play, and have time in the sun;
- Aim to wear them out with fun activities;
- Going to bed maintaining your usual evening routine as much as possible with good sleep hygiene practices in place can be helpful;
- Practices such as avoiding screen time for 2 hours before bed and having a calming evening routine are helpful for many people. Many children are used to a simple routine such as dinner, bath, brush teeth, change into pajamas, story, and bed;
- During the night when your child wakes up wanting to eat, drink, or use the bathroom give them what they need and return them to bed with as little engagement as possible;

- Every time your child wakes up, simply return them to bed if it is still time to sleep;
- You may find your child becomes distressed waking up at night in a strange bed, comfort them and return them to bed with as little disruption as possible;
- Try to keep the lighting low, a Gro-Blind or similar block out blind can be helpful to keep light levels low;
- Keep the noise levels low and their energy levels low by removing over stimulating toys and eliminating access to screen time if they wake up during the night.

Chapter 12: Do I Need to Immunise my Child Before I go?

Travelling will expose you to new environments and potentially to new viruses and bacteria. In addition to ensuring you and your child's vaccinations are up to date, you may want to consider taking immune supports prior to, and during your trip if you are concerned.

You can talk to your paediatrician in advance about using probiotics, vitamins, natural health supplements (for example, garlic, olive leaf extract, turmeric), or even just ensure you are eating nutritious food and skip the junk food as this will help to maintain your health while travelling.

Some areas have recommended vaccinations; the Australian Government's Smart Traveller website provides a good overview and you are able to search by destination for recommended vaccinations and precautions.

http://smartraveller.gov.au/guide/all-travellers/health/Pages/health-checks-and-vaccinations.aspx

Some countries will actually require proof of vaccination for yellow fever and will not allow entry without the vaccination. For a list of countries and their yellow fever vaccination requirements you can visit:

http://www.who.int/ith/2016-ith-county-list.pdf

Some vaccinations are quite expensive and are not covered by government vaccination schedule funding. The cost of this should be added to your holiday budget.

I do recommend you discuss any vaccinations and potential risks with your paediatrician and travel doctor, as requirements can change.

A Travel First Aid kit can be purchased from a travel doctor. These contain prescribed antibiotics, painkillers, and fluid replacements in addition to bandages and items typically found in a First Aid kit. These can be a literal lifesaver if you are travelling rurally and are unable to access medical services, the kit can provide support until you are able to reach the nearest doctor or hospital.

You certainly don't want to take unnecessary medications. If you are greatly concerned about potential side effects or interactions of medications on your child, you must discuss these with your doctor and you may need to change your travel plans to avoid certain areas, such as areas known for malaria.

Seek the advice of a travel doctor before finalising your travel plans. Depending on where you are travelling to, your travel doctor may recommend typhoid, cholera, and rabies vaccination. Keep in mind that some vaccinations are administered over a long period of time, with multiple doses and you may need a year or more to complete them, for example, Hepatitis B immunisations are administered over an extended time period. This should be factored into the timeline you have for your trip.

Some vaccinations will need to be repeated depending on when the initial vaccination was administered; for example, tetanus should be repeated every 10 years in adults, (**https://www.cdc.gov/features/tetanus/index.html**).

I worked with an occupational therapist who was bitten by a monkey while she was feeding them and she had fortunately had rabies vaccinations prior to her trip, she still had to receive medical treatment for rabies after the bite however it greatly helped her recover quickly. It is very easy to think it won't happen to you however monkey populations throughout tourist areas are used to being hand fed despite the warning signs and often no longer fear humans.

Meaning accidental bites (thinking your holding food and biting your fingers/ hand) is now increasingly common.

A close friend in high school suffered a severe accidental bite from a wombat when hand feeding it at a petting zoo in Sydney. These types of accidents are surprisingly quite common.

If you travel to an exotic location, or if you are spending time with animals, discuss the risks of parasitical infections with your doctor as it may be required that you deworm your family upon your return home.

While we don't like to think about them, parasitic worms are common in some areas of the world, and if you have pets you will be familiar with the practice of frequently deworming your pets and family. So if you have had contact with animals on your trip it is worth considering. If you have unusual symptoms following a trip, changes in appetite or loss of weight, it can be caused by worms or other parasites. Consult your doctor immediately and remember to discuss with them where you travelled.

You may need to check your children for ticks and leeches if you are in areas known to be affected by them.

The World Health Organization estimates that up to 20 percent of nutritional intake is lost when a child is host to parasitic worms*.

---

* More information:

http://worldwithoutworms.uwaterloo.ca/why.html

For more detailed information:

http://www.who.int/elena/titles/bbc/deworming/en/

Chapter 13: General Safety Considerations for International Travel

Online government travel advisories provide up-to-date general safety information on the countries you are travelling to. Pay special attention to factors such as elections and weather, as these can cause significant disturbance to an otherwise wonderful, peaceful trip.

Be prepared for the weather where you are staying, be aware of the signs of heat stroke, check for wet seasons if you are staying in a monsoon area, check for cyclone and hurricane seasons.

Be aware of foodborne illness and travel with a medical kit. Mild food poisoning is very common.

After using sauce from the table on my rice while in Cambodia, I ended up with severe food poisoning. The tour couldn't stop, so I was on a boat, a bus, a ferry, walking, another boat, then another bus while clutching a plastic bag. I ended up in a hospital in a small fishing village in Vietnam, on New Year's Eve, by myself, with the tour guide translating from English to Cambodian, his friend then translating from Cambodian to Vietnamese to the nurse, who then informed the doctor who told the nurse, who told the friend, who told the tour guide, who told me. It was a total mess.

When I looked up at the window, the window was filled with little faces who were all there to see the sick "white" woman. I can laugh a lot about it now. It took me more than a month to recover and following multiple courses of antibiotics it was only after the doctor prescribed probiotics that I started to improve. I am lucky. I know people who developed parasitic infections that ended in having permanent lifelong damage.

Here are a few basic food safety rules, (though there are no guarantees):

1. Avoid eating from street vendors;
2. Avoid using sauces kept on restaurant tables;
3. Check overall cleanliness of the venue;
4. Eat hot, cooked food;
5. Eat food that can be peeled;
6. Avoid dairy foods, particularly in countries without refrigeration;
7. Drink bottled water and check the seal;
8. Wash your hands well and use hand disinfectant;
9. Bring snacks with you from home in case you cannot find suitable food;
10. You can check online for ratings and read comments about the restaurant before you go;
11. If you can't drink the water don't use it to brush your teeth, and do not use the ice in your drink.

If you do get ill, seek medical help. Sipping flat soda or lemonade is a way to rehydrate if you are unable to access rehydration powders.

Religious festivals and public holidays may lead to widespread service shutdowns, so be sure to take note if these will be occurring during your trip. For instance, you may need to stock up on any special dietary needs in advance as stores and restaurants may be closed, or you may find public transport is not available on these days.

Australian Government Link:

http://www.smartraveller.gov.au

United Kingdom Government Link:

https://www.gov.uk/foreign-travel-advice

United States of America Government Link:

https://travel.state.gov/content/travel.html

Travelling with medication:

Australian Government Link:

https://www.homeaffairs.gov.au/trav/ente/brin/can-i-bring-it-back/can-i-bring-it-back-medicine/can-i-bring-medicine-back

United Kingdom Government Link:

https://www.gov.uk/travelling-controlled-drugs

United States of America Government Link:

https://help.cbp.gov/app/answers/detail/a_id/1160/~/traveling-with-medication

Chapter 14: Tips for Car Travel

Depending on your child, car travel might be blissful, a nightmare, or anywhere in between.

On many of our long car trips around Australia, my sister would fall asleep only to reawaken after we arrived at our destination. In comparison, my son would scream for hours until he finally slept from exhaustion ... until we discovered the iPad. Once he was given this, he would quietly watch his favourite show and we didn't have any further extended screaming bouts. It wasn't that he was car sick, or affected by the motion in anyway. Our active boy just did not like being restrained in his car seat. Once he was older and able to look outside the window, talk with us in the car, and listen to music or a story on CD he no longer had to rely on the iPad in the car to manage his boredom.

If your child is prone to motion sickness, make sure they have plenty of proprioception prior to getting into the car. Make sure they do not overeat before getting into the car. Small meals will be more easily tolerated if they become nauseous during the trip. Experiment with your child to find the position in the car that is easier for them. Some find sitting beside the window with a little fresh air helps, others prefer to sit in the center so they can see straight out the front window.

Just remember the regulations restricting young children from sitting in the front seat and ensure everyone is wearing their seatbelts and sitting in an age and weight appropriate seat.

Avoid changing your child's diet right before a long car trip. You might end up having upset stomachs for the whole trip.

If your children become easily bored in the car here are a few tips to help you think of some ideas that may work with your children:

- Make a "lucky dip" of cheap toys as presents or prizes;
- Special diet safe treats and snacks;
- Electronic devices, such as music players or DVD players;
- Music CDs;
- Activity books such as colouring books, puzzle books, or reading books;
- Create a wrapped gift pack for your child. Our first plane trip with mum, before planes were equipped with individual screens for movies and games, mum wrapped up a new pencil case with pencils and lollies and a colouring book, which kept us busy for quite a while. What is interesting is that over 20 years later I still remember it, so it clearly made quite an impression on me;
- Take frequent breaks especially at parks where your children can run with a ball, climb play equipment, and you can relax;
- During your rest breaks you can take advantage of this time by including physical play, particularly climbing, hanging, pushing and pulling on play equipment, if you can find a local park;
- If you cannot find a local park for your rest break, encourage your child to help by carrying heavy objects, for example, if you are going into and out of a coffee shop ask your child to carry a bag filled with activity toys or some books to give it some weight (up to 10 percent of your child's body weight);
- Provide your child with "heavy work" for their mouth by giving them thick shakes, fruit purees, jellies, or icy drinks to drink through a straw. Curly or thin straws also increase the resistance when sucking through them. Resistance whistles, available on

amazon.com or on sensorytools.com, can be great fun while outdoors and provide resistance while blowing which is helpful for calming children;

- Chewies made from safe plastic, or crunchy and chewy foods can provide good oral input that is calming and organising for your child's sensory systems;
- Provide an iPad or electronic device with DVDs, Leap Pads, music, or games. I do recommend you keep this until other activities such as colouring books, reading books, photo albums, singing together, or listening to music in the car have been exhausted, as these can be engrossing for children and you may find it challenging to transition them off a device once it has been given;
- Portable DVD players are affordable if you are not able to purchase iPads or similar. Ensure you have car chargers or additional batteries for any devices you are taking along. If your child is particularly attached to any CD or DVD, carrying a back up copy can be extremely helpful, especially if your child has not yet learnt how to be gentle with them;
- Make sure your child is physically comfortable during the trip. You may want to take along extra towels, changes of clothes, or a waterproof cover for the car seat in case of spilt drinks, toileting accidents, or even unexpected water play at parks along the way;
- Plan where you are seating your children. You probably already do this automatically knowing which of your children sit together better for longer periods of time. You may need to rotate your seating arrangement if your children disturb each other, in order to avoid one child becoming overly irritated with another;
- Plan what time of day you will be driving. If your child is particularly difficult in the car, consider if they will sleep through it if you drive at night;

- Make sure you have your sensory tool kit well stocked. Warmed toys or heat packs in the shape of toys, weighted toys, or vibrating cushions can be calming. Behind the seat organisers can be helpful in keeping your child's tools accessible and arranged;
- An over sun visor CD organiser can be helpful to manage CD/DVDs on the trip. I do not recommend leaving rented or borrowed items with your children, unless they are being handled by an adult, as it is extremely easy for these items to end up underfoot and broken in a car.

If your child refuses to remain seated while you are driving, you may be eligible to have a device prescribed by your paediatrician and an occupational therapist that will prevent your child from undoing the seatbelt. There are a number of serious implications when using such a device, and you will need to adhere to their recommendations to ensure your child's safety and they meet legal requirements that change from time to time.

Ensure that child locks are activated on your car doors.

If you are thinking about what to provide for snacks during road trips remember, when packing snacks for your road trip it can be tempting to fill the car with sugar, food colourings, and preservative laden "fun" treats. You could pack some sandwiches, tubs of noodles, muffins, or even pies to make it a healthier and cheaper trip. If you can avoid the drive-through, you will save money and be providing a healthier option to your children. If they need the toy, supply your own little toy or surprise with their packed foods, this way you have control over the toy's suitability for your child. For example, a quiet, blowing toy would be a great addition to your trip.

A good supply of crunchy and chewy foods that do not give you a sudden sugar rush and subsequent crash will help your child to maintain their energy levels, and ultimately will help avoid some problematic behaviours.

Here are some ideas to get you started:

- Sweet date balls;
- Crunchy vegetables in hummus dip;
- Crunchy fruit slices such as apples;
- Melon balls, berries;
- Dehydrated fruit strips;
- Banana chips (you can also get apple and pineapple);
- Dried cereals (you can make homemade granola);
- Drinking fluids through a thin straw;
- Drink fruit purees through a straw;
- Nuts (if allowed);
- Dried seeds (such as pepitas);
- Corn chips and dips like guacamole or corn relish.

If you are stopping for food at a restaurant or café, having a pre-prepared backpack that you can grab as you leave the car with your child's favourite snacks and activities can be helpful while you are waiting for your meals.

Roadside bathrooms can be a challenge for children with sensory issues, particularly if they are sensitive to smells. They can often be very cold, breezy, and dark, with insects, and often have icy cold water to wash hands with, wet floors, and dirty floors, walls and sinks.

A public bathroom can be a sensory sensitive or sensory seekers biggest challenge of the day.

Here are a few tips to give you some ideas of how you might approach this situation:

- Prepare a story in advance;
- Remind your child of what to expect;

- If your child is noise sensitive ensure you bring along their noise reducing tools.

NEVER allow your child to go into a public bathroom alone while travelling. The bathroom layout is unfamiliar and there is the risk of strangers. Even if the facility is empty it is common for public bathrooms in Australia and other countries not to have toilet seats, there are a variety of toilet paper dispensers and some of these can be very difficult to get paper from. The texture of the paper will likely be very different from what you are able to access at home, or they may not be any toilet paper available. It is common for sinks not to have working taps and for bins to be overflowing, or for there to be no bin at all. Hand driers can be extremely loud or may not work at all.

In addition to this, many public bathrooms are now equipped with specialised lighting to reduce the risk of drug use within the facility, creating a further change for your child to cope with. This could lead your child to panic in this unfamiliar, cold, often poorly lit environment.

Bring along a bag with the following:

- Toilet paper;
- Wet wipes;
- Hand sanitiser;
- Water bottle for rinsing hands as it is common for sinks not to work in public bathrooms;
- You may also want to bring along soap as an alternative to hand sanitiser if your child has sensitive skin;
- Hand towel for drying hands, you can use paper kitchen towels as a disposable option or a small face washer or hand towel as a reusable option.

If your child insists on sitting down, consider: can you bring along a child's toilet seat insert? That way they are not sitting directly on the toilet bowl, as public bathrooms often don't have seats.

Chapter 15: Preparing for Going on a Boat

If you are concerned how your child may react to being on a boat you can try taking a short ferry ride. For example, in Sydney Harbour you can take a 10-minute ferry ride across the harbour from Circular Quay to Luna Park on a full-sized ferry. This is an excellent, short introduction to being on a boat that gives you the opportunity to take photos for your storybook. It also gives you a quick insight into how well your child is able to tolerate being on a boat without finding yourself trapped for hours on end with no options available.

Use short trips to identify challenges and problem solve around them. Repeating the trip and gradually increasing the length of trips by choosing different destinations allows you to identify what solutions work well for your family.

The repeated exposure to being on the boat will help reduce your child's anxiety and build tolerance as they become more familiar with this environment.

Autism on the Seas is based in the USA and provides cruises for adults and families living with autism, Down syndrome and other related disabilities. They offer financial assistance. Their Facebook page is filled with lots of very happy faces.

http://www.facebook.com/autismontheseas

If you are planning to go on a boat discuss and trial under your pediatrician's supervision anti-nausea medications prior to the trip. If you prefer to avoid medication ginger has been found reduce nausea for some people.

Chapter 16: What can I do if my Plans Fall Apart?

The more you travel the more you will know things don't always go to plan, which isn't so bad if you're travelling without children and don't mind sleeping on your backpack in an airport. However, when travelling with children, having a backup plan for everything is wise.

Arriving at your hotel to find they don't have your booking and are booked out is tough but happens, ensure you have the phone numbers of some alternatives. Having a handbag stolen or even just losing a favourite toy can derail an entire trip, with children being unable to sleep, becoming grumpy and agitated.

You may need to be prepared to spend the day (or days) in a hotel because of stomach bugs, bad weather, or unexpected national events. Having a good supply of indoor activities such as games, books, electronic devices, or DVDs as a backup can be helpful.

You may need to split up and do different activities, or even sleep in different shifts at times if your child is unwell or is unable to settle during your trip.

Be prepared, you might have to decide that things aren't working out right now and just go home early, for example, if you're camping and it's raining.

This is where having travel insurance is vital. You can receive personalised advice on which level of cover is most suitable for your needs from an insurance company.

From lost luggage, cancelled flights, illness and accidents, travel insurance will help cover you for the losses and costs you incur additionally many companies provide helpful advice.

Australian's can access helpful travel advice from:

www.smarttraveller.gov.au

Australians can also register their travel plans on the smart traveller website, which allows the government to notify you or your family during an emergency.

Before travelling, I provided my family with certified copies of my passport, insurance information, ticket information, and itinerary and when I relocated overseas on a long term basis I added my parents as agents onto one of my bank accounts so that they were able to access my account in case of emergency.

If you have a trusted family member, friend, or even your solicitor you may like to provide them with copies of your paperwork so that they can act on your behalf in case of an emergency, particularly if you are travelling for a longer period of time.

Chapter 17: What can I do if People React to my Child?

There is certainly no perfect answer to this question and no ideal reaction, though these situations can cause a lot of distress for families.

The reality is that we live in a global environment with people travelling constantly, however while you are travelling you will often find that people do not share the same values, attitudes, awareness, or education as yourself.

You may find that people openly stare at a person with a disability. As a parent or carer of a child or person who has a disability, you may find that people approach you and ask questions or make comments that you find inappropriate and hurtful. Or offer unsolicited advice and comments.

I suggest you ignore anyone who makes comments or stares if your child's behaviours are attracting attention. Do remember that you have the choice whether or not you take offence at comments made to you. You do have the choice over how you feel and how you respond to comments made. You can choose to let go of offence. You are responsible only for your own actions and reactions.

Remember, given language and cultural differences you cannot always be sure if someone is simply curious or if they are intending to offend you.

I like what Barry Neil Kaufman proposes in his Option Institute Training when he says about people, "they are doing the best they can with the knowledge and skills they possess at this time" and "you did the best you could with the knowledge and skills you had at the time", how beautifully freeing is that thought?

So how does that translate to real life? Let's look at an example, someone rudely yelling at you to tell your child to be quiet when you are waiting in line at the supermarket. You could respond, "I am sorry he/she is disturbing you. He/she is doing the best he/she can right now." Then make an active choice not to take offence. You may want to create a card that says, "I apologise if my child was disturbing you" and then explains your child's disability in simple language, (this could be translated if you are travelling to a country where you do not speak the local language). You are assuming a non-judgmental attitude in response to others. You are modelling the behaviour you expect your own children to display and how you hope you and your child will be treated by other adults in response.

As a parent flying with young children I have had people look at my toddler and baby while I was boarding and make remarks about how unlucky they were to be having so many babies on board. These people are simply not part of my life. I let their comments pass by and we had a lovely, safe flight.

Tell yourself that this person is doing the best they can to look after themselves, and you in turn are doing the best you can to look after yourself and your family. Then push the matter from your mind. Their attitudes do not affect you and certainly should not affect your enjoyment of your holiday that you have worked, planned, and saved for.

I have used this approach frequently in the playground in regards to special needs children I am with. Other children have inquisitively said, "What is wrong with her?" "Why doesn't she talk?", "Why does she look like that?", "Is she dumb?" and more. Their questions and attitudes may reflect those of their culture and family or they could simply be poorly, worded genuine interest.

You can use this approach when talking with children who can come up with their innocent yet blatant questions and statements. An inquisitive child who typically lacks all subtly or the ability to be politically correct can best learn from a caring response that honours the child with the special need, "She is doing the best she can right now, how about we go and play with her?" or "She is doing the best she can right now, see how she is using signs to tell you what she wants? Let's go and talk with her." "See how she is making a beautiful drawing in the sand, would you like to ask her if you can join her?

In using this approach in this type of situation I have then heard the child who asked the original question repeating this to other children who have asked them what is wrong with her. Hearing that child then say to another child, "She is doing her best" and "She is doing the best she can" was beautiful. We can spread this non-judgmental attitude with our own. We don't judge the questioning child but rather show them how they can join the child and share their company in a respectful way. This is a great way to build an inclusive playground by showing children how to respond to differences in a positive way at a very young age.

Remember you don't always need to explain that your child has special needs, or go into the details of your child's disability, particularly to adults. Irritable, thoughtless, and rude people are simply not worth engaging with, and your lovely vacation time isn't necessarily the time to worry about campaigning for disability awareness or rights. You can absolutely take action when you get home. Letters to company executives can be quite effective especially since it is becoming less common for people to write a letter. Just make sure you take time to relax and enjoy your vacation.

If you are at home in your community it is absolutely worth educating companies and individuals on appropriate ways to be inclusive and how they can support your family. Attitudes are rapidly improving as people become more educated, and we are seeing wonderful improvements in how the community is becoming more aware of how they can support individual differences.

If you are offered unwanted, unsolicited advice a simple, "Thanks so much" and turn back to what you are doing. Don't let people disrupt your holiday.

Being prepared in advance can help you maintain your equilibrium when something like this gets thrown in your face. I recommend if you are travelling with children that you actually role-play some scenarios with the whole family. What will you say or do if someone says something judgmental or hurtful?

You need to come up with a solution that you all feel comfortable with, that you feel will dispel a situation rather than create a confrontation so that you can go back to enjoying your trip as soon as possible. You can do this through stories and role-plays, which can help equip both children and adults to respond in an intentional manner instead of reacting from anxiety, hurt and fear.

Knowing your legal rights in the country you're visiting can be helpful to parents. I recommend you avoid verbal arguments wherever possible, and remember that in many countries it is not illegal to discriminate against a person with a disability, but it is illegal to swear in public or use rude gestures which could result in jail terms – and that's a really great way to ruin your holiday. So protect yourself by maintaining your sense of peace and do not engage with such people.

Ultimately ignoring and walking away may be the most suitable response, particularly in a foreign country.

To facilitate this, practising self-calming techniques for both children and adults can significantly help to reduce anxiety when placed in confrontational situations.

Chapter 18: How can I Create a Story Book for my Child?

This is a really simple process and there are a number of smartphone apps available that will help you. Though it really isn't necessary, if you have access to a computer and a printer you can create your own easily. You really don't need to be very technical to create a helpful story for your child.

1. Get images;
2. Create a simple text explaining what will happen;
3. Put together in a word document;
4. Save;
5. Print;
6. Laminate to ensure it will last.

1. Select relevant images and copy and paste into a word document (you might prefer to set the layout to landscape).

2. Develop a simple script. Aim for one sentence per page. Think about what you would like to tell your child about that image. For example, "We are going on an airplane" with an image of a plane as the title page. The first page might be of you all in your car with the text stating "we are going to drive to the airport", and go through each step until you have your image of the site you are visiting.

3. Print the document, you may like to laminate and bind it to create a longer lasting "book".

4. Email the document to yourself in case you lose the book on your travels, you can also save this as a PDF and view on your mobile using the acrobat reader app.

There are a number of apps designed to help with creating stories for your child. For example, Social Story Creator and Library allows you to take photos, type text, and record your voice reading the text so your child can independently read and listen to the story you have created for them.

It can be very helpful to add feelings to the story you are creating for your child. With one picture per line of text.

For example:

" I am going on an airplane"

"I feel excited and"

"I feel scared / anxious / angry"

"My mother (or name who will accompany the child) will sit beside me the whole time"

"I can breathe deeply if I feel upset"

"I can ask for the things I need using my pictures"

"I will be on the plane for 2 hours"

"Then I will get to …. (include something that your child can look forward to such as play at a park, swim, see grandma and so on).

Be sure to include:

How will you help your child manage their emotions during the flight?

What tools and toys will your child have access to on the flight?

The time frame for the trip that you expect.

What will happen if there are delays.

Chapter 19: How can I Prepare my Child for a Challenging Sensory Experience?

If you know your child will have difficulty with the noise from the plane engine, the crowds at the market, or the lights at a show, you can help prepare them for the experience. Knowing what will happen in advance and why is very important for preparing your child's nervous system.

You can help prepare your child by creating a storybook for them about the upcoming experience, as previously discussed. You can explain to them that you are going to be exposed to the sensory inputs, and clearly explain to them what they will experience and how long it will last. Also explain what supports you are providing to them to help them in this experience. We use one sentence per page.

An example of this would be: "We are going on a train. The train will be very busy, there will be a lot of people, there will be different smells, and there will be a lot of noise. We will be on the train for 15 minutes. It will feel like a long time. I will be with you the whole time. You can wear your hat and your sunglasses, you can listen to your favourite music on your player and wear your earphones. I have a handkerchief with your favourite smell (aromatherapy oil) on it. I have some chewing gum for you. When we get off the train we will..." Then give them their chosen reward – play at the park, a snack, or go for a piggyback ride on your back. Consider what you can offer in that environment.

The format I have found useful is:

1. What will you be doing?
2. Why are you doing it?
3. How long are you doing it for?
4. What challenge might they face?
5. What do you expect them to do?
6. What supports are available for them to use?

7. What can they look forward to after the experience? (reward/ positive reinforcement).

Providing proprioceptive input and oral input can help regulate your child's sensory systems.

Proprioception is the information from your joints, muscles, and connective tissues which tells your body about where you are in space. This is how you know where your body is and what it is doing without having to look at it.

To help prepare your child's central nervous system for a challenging sensory experience you can provide proprioceptive input. For example, if your child has difficulty sitting still during a long car trip, providing proprioceptive input in the form of heavy work, such as climbing, before getting back into the car after a break can help prepare your child's nervous system for being in the car.

Proprioceptive input such as firm massage, firm hugs, stretches, hanging from a pull up bar, climbing, pressure vests, weighted blankets, and weighted vests can be very calming for the central nervous system. Sucking a thick liquid through a straw such as a thick shake, or fruit puree, provides heavy work for the facial muscles.

Chewing is also considered to be calming and organising for the central nervous system. Chewy and crunchy foods provide heavy work for the oral muscles and jawbones.

An occupational therapist will be able to provide specific recommendations tailored to your child's specific sensory needs, and will work with you to determine which equipment and activities best help their sensory systems, as each child is unique.

Chapter 20: How can I Support my Child's Sensory System During a Challenging Sensory Experience?

During a challenging sensory experience your child will likely have a reduced capacity to listen and respond to instructions you provide. Be aware of this.

Keep your language simple, minimise demands.

Provide proprioception and deep pressure inputs.

You should know in advance what is helpful to your child and you can ensure you have your child's preferred sensory tools available for the trip.

For example, if your child has difficulty with loud noises, travelling on an airplane will be challenging due to the drone of the airplane engines, unexpected announcements, buzzers and noise from other passengers, and of course the bathroom noises which can be quite scary for any child.

Think ahead and problem solve any issues you see arising. Think of past trips and what worked well for your child, plan what you can do differently this trip to avoid any issues you faced in the past.

Calming Sensory Tips

- Listening to music;
- Noise reduction headphones;
- Massage;
- Bath or shower;
- Stroking a smooth object, for example a "pet rock";
- Time with pets;
- Exercise, for example doing twenty pushups or holding a plank position;
- Weighted blankets;
- Tent made from a blanket;

- Chewing gum or chewable objects such as chewy jewellery;
- Cold drink;
- Suck or chew ice, such as a water-based ice block;
- Drink thick fluid through a straw;
- Self stimulation – "stims" or "isms";
- Climb – (children can go to the park, young adults and adults can go rock climbing);
- Use a chin up bar;
- Yoga or Pilates;
- Hot water bottle;
- Star jumps;
- Martial arts – "katas";
- Skip with a rope;
- Jog up stairs or on the spot;
- Dance along with a children's music video;
- Laugh – use a trigger such as a funny comic, video or even just start laughing and see where it takes you
- Sing or hum – this increases oxygen available and can help change your mood and your child's mood.

Helpful resources during a challenging sensory experience

- Pressure vests;
- Weighted blankets and vests;
- Stretching exercises and games;
- Weight bearing exercises and games;
- Blowing, sucking, or chewing oral motor toys;
- Favourite music;
- Sound therapy systems;
- Noise reducing headphones;
- Sunglasses;
- Hat;
- Chewing gum or chewy lollies, dried fruits, or dehydrated vegetables;

- Wet wipes, spare towel, spare clothing – especially for tactile sensitive children;
- Favourite toy – to distract and comfort your child with.

During a challenging sensory experience reduce the expectations and demands on your child – for instance you might not expect your child to greet the aircrew as you enter and exit the airplane, you might allow your child to avoid eye contact during the flight. You are allowing your child to avoid sensory overload during this challenging experience.

Chapter 21: How can I Help my Child Recover from a Meltdown?

While reducing the number of meltdowns is the priority there will be times where this is not possible and they do experience a meltdown.

It can be helpful to provide reassurance that you are there with them and that everything is okay. Use simple language. If they are unable to understand your words your calm tone and reassuring presence will help remind them you are there.

When they are ready to receive it provide proprioception by giving them a firm hug or squeeze their hand for reassurance. Avoid light touch, especially if they are touch sensitive.

Provide a quiet environment with less visual and auditory stimulation. Noise reducing headphones can be very helpful if you are unable to change your environment (for example if you are on public transport).

Try not to place additional demands on your child until they are fully recovered, if possible.

Show your child that you are calm. This requires you to manage your breathing, posture, tone of voice and facial expressions. Meltdowns can be very frightening for the child and their family members. Try and find a strategy that helps you to remain calm and practice it regularly so when you find yourself in a stressful situation you are able to automatically use your strategies that you know work for you for example, using breathing techniques, worry beads, visualization, progressive muscle relaxation have been found to be helpful for managing stress.

Ensure you do not punish your child - a meltdown is completely out of their control.

Provide a slow return to activities to avoid further sensory-based reactions. You may need to reduce your expectations of how much your child is able to do for the next few hours. For example, If you are at the shopping centre you may need to return home and return to the store on another day.

Following the meltdown you may want to provide your child a sip of water; however I suggest avoiding a full meal or large drinks until they have fully recovered.

When you and your child have recovered it is important to determine what triggered the meltdown. Remembering there is likely a lot going on in your child's sensory world that you are not aware of. For instance there may be uncomfortable sounds that you are simply unable to hear, or an event from the previous day may be still adding to the sensory load they are experiencing.

Following the event keeping a diary to record what happened before, during and after a meltdown can be helpful. If your child is able to communicate verbally ask them what felt overwhelming? What helped you feel better? Keeping a record of what strategies your child found helpful will allow you to ensure you have those tools and resources on hand and are able to communicate what works for your child to other family members or school staff. This will help you to track the frequency of meltdowns and evaluate if the strategies you are using are reducing the frequency.

Showing your child you will continue to support them is essential. Continue to provide modifications to the environment where possible for example: Choosing to go to the shopping centre during the "sensory hour" where the store does not play music to help reduce the overwhelming experiences in the store.

Continue to provide tools (such as sun glasses, hat or hooded jacket for light sensitivity, chewy tools or weighted toys) and use the strategies you have found helpful to reduce sensory meltdowns for your child where possible.

Most importantly for reducing future meltdowns ensuring clear communication with your child will allow them to understand what is happening. If your child is non-verbal you may need to review their communication system to assist them to communicate with you what they need and when they are feeling overwhelmed.

Provide choice and control over the experience where possible, keeping in mind that it must be age and developmentally appropriate. This will help to reassure your child and help reduce future meltdowns.

If you child has a favourite tool, toy or routine that helps calm them down ensure they are able to access these resources with your support and as it becomes age appropriate ensure they are able to access these tools independently. This will help your child learn to self manage their sensory needs; with the aim to reduce the meltdowns they experience and help them to eventually be able to recover from meltdowns independently as they grow into adulthood.

Create a small calm down kit that can be carried with you easily. Having easy access to something to bite on, stoke, smell, squeeze, stretch, something that feels heavy, their favourite music or toy can help before, during and after a meltdown.

Chapter 22: What are Some Signs of Sensory Overload?

It can be difficult to determine when your child is reaching the point of sensory overload. This could come across as a sudden change in the behaviour of a child who has been exposed to sensory inputs such as, spinning on a swing, jumping, or even just travelling on a new form of transport.

Watch out for the following signs:

- If your child becomes unexpectedly quiet;
- Has nausea or vomits;
- Has a headache;
- Is unusually drowsy or falls asleep unexpectedly;
- Has a change in their skin colour;
- If your child loses coordination skills and becomes clumsy.

It is important to know your child's individual signs of being overwhelmed so that you can help your child before they reach sensory overload.

How does your child behave when they are overwhelmed?
- Do they become disorganised?
- Do they become irritable?
- Do they become quieter?
- Do they start staring?
- Do they start rocking?
- Do they self harm?

Talk to your child's occupational therapist if you are concerned about their sensory processing. The therapist will help you design a protocol to implement if your child reaches sensory overload. It is best to remove any overwhelming sensory inputs before they reach this stage.

Chapter 23: What can Contribute to Sensory Overload?

Having more sensory information than you can process causes sensory overload. The amount of sensory input that can cause sensory overload varies from person to person, and will change over time.

A child who is unwell, is experiencing stress, or changes will be more susceptible to overload than they might typically be.

Light touch, particularly unexpected light touch like tickling, can be challenging for children who have tactile sensitivity.

Tactile sensitive children may find changes in clothing or food textures can be difficult to manage and this can lead to sensory overload.

Visual inputs such as flashing lights, spinning images, overly decorated rooms, or clutter can lead to visual overload.

Loud, prolonged noise and even sounds with a particular pitch or tone can easily lead to overload.

Food sensitivities can heighten overall sensitivity and irritability, reducing your child's overall tolerance for sensory inputs and demands in areas they may not be typically sensitive to.

Being unwell can reduce your child's tolerance for sensory inputs.

It is important to know your child's triggers. Is your child sensitive to movements such as spinning? Are they sensitive to visual inputs such as flashing lights or sharp edges?

If your child is tactile sensitive then clothing labels, rough fabrics, seams on socks and clothing, or uneven edges of shoes can be irritating. If your child has vestibular sensitivity, they may be afraid of heights or being off the ground.

Is your child a sensory seeker or sensory craver? These children can switch from being in a seeking state to a very disorganised sensory state very quickly when they become overloaded with sensory inputs.

This can be challenging to interpret, as a seeking child may seem to be calming down when in fact they may have become drowsy or unusually quiet due to sensory overload.

This is where an occupational therapist can greatly help a family in determining their child's individual triggers, or signs of sensory overload and create a tailored plan to assist your child to manage their challenging sensory experiences.

Chapter 24: Tips for Reducing Sensory Overload

Reduce, or if possible remove, sensory inputs. For example, put your child in a pram and cover the pram with a blanket to remove visual sensory inputs. For a child who has tactile sensitivity, hug or deep pressure massage, wrap in a towel or blanket, or use a pressure vest to help reduce light touch. Hug your child and gently rock. Avoid light touch such as stroking their arm as this can be irritating for a person with touch sensitivity.

Provide 'heavy work' such as carrying a sand or water bucket at the beach, wearing a back pack with a load, or climb or hang on a climbing frame at the park.

Rhythmic, slow visual inputs can be calming such as a lava lamp or calming glitter bottle.

Oral input by chewing on a therapy chew tool (there is now a huge range of these tools available in different shapes and different levels of firmness) or a large wad of chewing gum can be helpful because it provides deep pressure.

Music, being placed in a quiet area, white noise or sound therapy listening programs can help block out triggering sounds for children who are sensitive to noise.

Older children can be taught to use tools such as tapping, self massage, fidget toys, or exercise such as weight lifting to help manage their sensory systems.

Having choice and control over their sensory experiences you have in your life can make a major difference in your ability to cope with what is happening. Parents can help by providing choices. For example choice of fabrics for clothes but also bed sheets, pillow cases and blankets, shampoos, soaps, laundry detergents, toothpastes, options for flossing teeth, control over lighting and noise levels. For instance the sound of a ticking clock for an individual with sound sensitivity can be very difficult to cope with, and may even affect their ability to fall asleep. Having a digital clock is a simple alternative.

Knowing the order activities are going to be completed in, knowing what is going to happen and for how long can greatly help coping skills, reduce anxiety and reduce sensory overload.

Stretching and strength exercises such as yoga and Pilates can be extremely helpful for managing sensory needs among their other health benefits. Pilates and yoga provide proprioceptive input and can help meet the body's need for movement without overwhelming for those who are sensitive to fast movements or find games / sports with their complex rules difficult to follow.

Teach your child a simple progressive relaxation technique such as, squeeze your shoulders up, press them down, squeeze your hands into tight fists, release.

The basis of this relaxation technique is to first tense muscles then release the muscle as you work your way around your body.

Practising this in a quiet place will help the technique to be more effective over time, especially when you really need it as an escape.

You may prefer to sit or lay down during the relaxation.

Remember you should never feel any pain or discomfort from the process of the relaxation exercise.

You can adapt the technique to your own preferences, start where you are most comfortable, you can work on one of your arms and legs at a time or you may prefer to do both legs or both arms together. Do what works for you.

For each body part move your awareness to the area, tense the area, hold the tension for 2 – 4 seconds then relax.

Keep breathing calmly throughout as you follow the sequence:

1. Right foot
2. Left foot
3. Right calf
4. Left calf
5. Right thigh
6. Left thigh
7. Hips
8. Stomach
9. Chest
10. Back
11. Right arm and hand
12. Left arm and hand
13. Neck and shoulders
14. Face

You can find more information about progressive relaxation at the following addresses:

http://www.anxietybc.com/sites/default/files/MuscleRelaxation.pdf

http://www.helpguide.org/mental/stress_relief_meditation_yoga_relaxation.htm

http://www.amsa.org/healthingthehealer.musclerelaxation.cfm

This final address includes a link to a 9-minute recording you can listen to as you practise the technique.

https://www.hws.edu/studentlife/counseling_relax.aspx

Chapter 25: How can I Reduce my Stress Levels?

This topic could, of course, be a whole book on its own, so I will briefly mention some techniques that you can investigate. It is important that you find a stress management technique that works for you, and that you practise this daily.

It takes a great deal of mental strength to deal with the additional stresses travel can bring when you are travelling with children. Some of you may have experienced any or all of the following while travelling: fatigue, motion sickness, jet lag, loss of luggage, long periods of time in transit, missed connections, lost papers, illness and more. In addition to this you have the usual demands of parenthood with mouths to be fed and children's whims to cater to.

There will be times that you may even regret taking your trip and become stressed about being so stressed! It is possible to develop your attitude "muscles", and you can find that many of the little things stop bothering you. I really enjoyed reading Jack Canfield's book, "Don't Sweat the Small Stuff."

Planning your trip thoroughly and going through the worst-case scenarios before you travel can greatly reduce your stress levels if things do go wrong.

Manage your expectations. Expect to wait in lines, have bad weather, and have tired, cranky children and adults. Expect to lose things, to find tourist attractions closed without notice, and the traffic to the airport to take three times longer than it should. That's simply part of your experience when you travel. It won't all happen at the same time, and something won't go wrong every trip; but sometimes you simply have to shrug things off. Remember that hotels will often post items to you, you can get travel documents reissued, skipping a meal won't ruin your whole trip, and you can backup your photos.

Backups of all your essentials can be invaluable:

- Photocopies of all your travel documents;
- Special foods for children on restricted diets;
- Favourite clothes for children who have tactile sensitivity or inflexibilities;
- Preferred toys, DVDs etc.;
- Spare batteries and chargers stored in separate bags so that a little thing like a lost bag doesn't derail your entire trip.

A computer virus caused me to lose all of my photos from my trips, including China, Thailand, Cambodia, and Vietnam, with both my computer and backup drive damaged. I now have multiple backups and email my favourite photos to myself. A cloud backup for storing your files offsite can provide additional protection to a physical external drive.

Think about your plan B and try not to be overly attached to your predetermined schedule.

Prepare for the worst and turn your focus to the benefits of your trip: how great you are going to feel; how wonderful it will be to have this shared experience as a family; how great it will be for your kids to remember going to the theme park, or the beach, or the forest; and how you will have the photos to remember your trip.

Before you travel start practising meditation, such as yoga and progressive relaxation, daily. These practices can be very helpful but you do need to develop your skills in using them before they will become an effective stress management tool. When you start out, your focus is typically on how to complete the process; once you practise regularly you will be able to quickly use meditation to achieve some relaxation, even when on a noisy airplane.

Many people find prayer to be extremely beneficial in their daily lives irrespective of religious affiliation.

Tapping is an unusual technique that I have found to be very helpful in quickly diffusing distressing feelings and thoughts. There are free guides to help you learn about this technique at:

www.thetappingsolution.com

As effective as relaxation techniques are, they simply won't be effective if you are trying them for the first time while having missed your airport connection, and have three hungry kids pulling at you. Relaxation techniques should be practiced regularly while you are calm so you can automatically start using the strategy when you are in a stressful situation.

Calming music can be very helpful in setting a calm tone. Upbeat, uplifting music can also help lift you up when having low moods or when feeling tired.

Filling your music device or playlists with music you already know to be effective at improving your mood and decreasing your stress levels will make a big difference.

I personally find listening to motivational messages can also greatly help reduce my stress levels by helping me to reset my focus on the positive aspects of what is happening, without allowing the stressful parts to become overwhelming. Having music, messages, scriptures, or even a pre-recorded message to yourself preloaded into your phone or other devices can make a big difference.

You need to find what works for you, have it ready, and make it easy to access. When in a stressful situation people will typically take the "path of least resistance", meaning we will do what is easiest in the situation even if it isn't necessarily the "best" decision. So make it easy to access what works for you.

- Can you take time out to do some exercise? Even just running fast on the spot can change your mood;
- Can you lock yourself in the bathroom and play pumped up music for five minutes through your earphones?
- Do you need to get some fresh air? Even just opening the windows letting in fresh air and light can help lift your mood if you are feeling down;
- Can your partner or friend watch the children to give you a rest?
- Do you need to talk kindly to yourself?
- Think of what you can do that works for you before you take your trip. Make sure you have packed any equipment or resources you need: journals, music, earphones, or bubble bath.
- Visualise yourself being calm, happy, and coping with any challenge that comes up. See having a wonderful trip.

Sound therapy is often reported by practitioners to be helpful in stress management for both adults and children. There are a number of different types of sound therapy programs available on the market, so you may like to do some research to ensure the best match for yourself and your family. Some programs can only be accessed through licensed therapists. A program accessible to the general public is **www.soundtherapyinternational.com**

Do remember to build rest breaks into your daily life and in your holidays. It is easy to overbook your schedule and end up feeling exhausted after a vacation. With so many exciting things to se and do on a holiday in a limited time frame this is one of my biggest challenges.

Chapter 26: Questions to ask when Booking Accommodation

Based on your child's needs you may want to find out about the following:

- Windows – are the windows sealed or can they be opened?
- Check the size of the bed, particularly if you are planning to pack waterproof sheets for your child;
- Is there a kitchenette and what facilities are included?
- Is there a fridge available?
- Check if there is a swimming pool. If so, is there a life guard?
- What floor are you being booked onto?
- Is there a balcony? If so, can it be locked with a removable key? (So that you can lock the door and then store the key safely);
- How long does it take to drive from the airport to the accommodation?
- How long does it take to drive from the hotel to the attractions you are planning to visit? Distance on a map can be very deceiving. Local traffic jams can cause very short distances to take hours to travel.

If your child is sensitive to sounds you may find your room location to be problematic if you are located near lifts, slamming doors, music, or roadways. Sound therapy, noise reducing headphones, and white noise machines can be helpful if you are not able to change your room.

If you are interested in having your child minded while at the accommodation, you can check with the hotel in advance if they offer this service.

Local therapy services at your destination may be able to provide recommendations regarding child care services in the area that cater to children who have special needs. Online support groups may be able to provide personal experience regarding particular services. Forums such as **expatwoman.com** provide an excellent support for families worldwide where you can post questions and search others questions and responses.

If you need help with your children you can request a nanny service to provide a staff member that accompanies your family. For example a mother's helper, for when you are visiting a theme park, to provide an extra pair of hands while you are juggling your things, and more importantly your children between attractions, shows, and rides.

Some therapy clinics offer holiday camps that your children may enjoy, so check the services available in the area before you travel in case you find you want to book any activities for your child in advance.

Chapter 27: Eating at a Restaurant

As a parent I am frequently frustrated when I go to a restaurant and look over the children's menu. There are often lovely healthy choices for adults; however, children's menus typically seem to be restricted to chicken nuggets, pizza, pasta, and fries. In our family we order meals for the adults and divide it to provide a portion to our two-year-old son. If this is not possible then we order an adult meal for him and take home the unused portion so that he can access the healthier options on the adult menu.

When you are booking your hotel you can ask the concierge for information, and do an online search for restaurants in the hotel and local area. Most restaurants will be able to provide basic foods, such as baked potatoes, salads, and fruit. Be careful with meat products as they can be marinated in ingredients they may not be willing to reveal or may not be aware of.

If your child has special dietary needs make your bookings at the restaurant in advance and discuss dietary restrictions.

If you are travelling to non-English speaking countries, have a list of foods and ingredients your child is allergic to in the local language so you can check these at restaurants and supermarkets.

In my travels I have found at some restaurants that many ingredients in the food were provided to the restaurant premixed and prepackaged. This means in some instances the staff do not always actually know the full list of ingredients of the food being served.

We are living in Dubai and our local supermarkets offer food packaged in French, German, Arabic, and English. To avoid specific ingredients I need to know how they appear printed in these languages as English is not always available.

When I lived in Singapore I frequently found it difficult to obtain vegetarian meals at my local eatery. I would ask in Mandarin and English for non-meat dishes and when I would receive my meal I would find meat in it. I would then return the meal and ask for no meat and they would reply "That is fish, it is not meat" or "That is chicken, it is not meat". It is an irritant for someone choosing to live a vegetarian lifestyle or wanting to eat less meat; however, such attitudes can have life threatening consequences when you have allergies.

If your child has severe food allergies ensure you have your medications with you whenever you are eating, as you may find that the staff do not respect your request or may not understand the implications of the allergen.

Chapter 28: How can I Maintain my Child's Special Diet on the Trip?

When you book your hotel accommodation ensure there is a refrigerator in the room.

If you have the option of booking a room with a kitchenette it will be much easier for you if you need to prepare special meals for your child.

There are many free meal planning resources available online. Planning ahead will help you reduce the stress around meal times, particularly while you are in a new area and will help save time and money.

Now stores are providing online shopping you may be able to have groceries delivered to your hotel depending on your location. Researching online before hand can save you considerable time and money particularly if you are able to pack lunches and snacks in your hotel room.

Our family has frequently stayed in holiday campsites renting cabins that came with fully equipped kitchens. This has made the trip so much more economical for our family, as campsite accommodation is more affordable than a hotel and being able to eat in the cabin greatly cut back on food costs.

For day trips carry a small esky or cooler bag with ice packs. I have found freezing water in ziplock bags has been an easy way to make disposable ice packs. Freezing a wet sponge and placing in a ziplock bag is an easy way to reduce leaking as the ice melts.

Check the area you will be staying in for stores that will sell foods that cater to your child's needs. For example, organic stores or health food stores typically carry gluten free/dairy free products. Fortunately around the world, major supermarkets are stocking these items more frequently.

Check restaurants near where you are planning to stay. Menus are often available online and you can call ahead to request your meals based on your dietary requirements. Making an advanced booking can ensure the restaurant is able to cater to your needs.

Do remember that some restaurants will not take bookings and some will not cater to special needs diets. By calling ahead you may have saved yourself a drive, and you can go elsewhere.

I have found preparing "whole" foods from scratch is the most effective way to avoid allergens. If you are a parent of a child with food sensitivities or allergies you will already be an expert at reading ingredient lists, and will be familiar with the different terms used by manufacturers for ingredients. This can be helpful when travelling.

When travelling I have frequently found food products without English ingredient lists. When I lived in Singapore our local supermarket provided products and the ingredients were typically printed in Chinese. In the UAE ingredient lists are always in Arabic, and often are also written in German and even French. English is not always available.

Depending on the country you are travelling to you may want to prepare for this by having your child's allergies written in the local language of the country you are visiting. You can then match this to any ingredient lists on products you want to buy when shopping.

A multi-cooker such as the "InstaPot" can help you cook an entire healthy meal in your hotel room. Depending on the county you are travelling to you may need to carry an power converter. These can usually be purchased at international airports if you forget to bring one.

Chapter 29: We Have a Kitchenette in our Holiday Accommodation. How can I Make it Safer?

To secure cupboards you can purchase cupboard locks that can be attached to the door handles without permanent attachments required.

Switch the stove, microwave, and kettle off at the wall when not in use. You may want to store toasters and kettles away out of reach when not in use as these can become temptation for a bored child.

Store medications, sharp knives, and cleaning equipment in a locked cupboard and take any other precautions you would usually take in your own home.

If there is a bar fridge, you may want to request hotel staff remove the contents (or do so yourself) to avoid having your child accessing the drinks and foods.

Take along electrical outlet covers if you use them at home, though remember, outlet's vary from country to country so if travelling internationally this may not be an option. You might try using masking tape to cover outlets if this is an issue for your child as it can be applied and removed without damage to the outlet. Though depending on your child it may only delay them for a moment as it is quite easily removed.

Chapter 30: Tips for Travelling to the Beach

Teach your child to swim – start now! I cannot emphasise this point enough. Every year children drown unnecessarily because they have not been equipped with basic water safety skills.

All children can learn some level of water safety skills. Additionally, you will find that children who have limited mobility will often have increased mobility while in the water and will get therapeutic benefits from swimming.

Water play is very therapeutic and many cities have swimming clubs dedicated to children who have special needs.

So many vacations involve water; swimming pools, beaches, lakes, dams, rivers, and spa baths. I strongly recommend you start teaching your child to swim as soon as possible, as it can take years to develop competence for some children. If your child already has the basics down, continue to increase their swimming skills.

All adults and older children should complete first aid and CPR training. If possible adults should complete swimming rescue training if you intend to holiday near water; learn the signs of the water, for example, how to identify rips and dangerous currents.

When at the beach only swim between the flags on patrolled beaches and avoid the rocks at all times. The life you save could be yours.

Ensure you provide a hat, sunblock, sun shirt, and drinking water to help prevent sunburn and heat stroke.

Ensure you identify which adult is responsible for supervising which child, particularly when in a group situation. Formally allocate supervision for a period of

time and then hand over to the next person at the agreed time.

It is very easy for groups to adopt a mentality where they assume someone else is watching the children; and a number of drowning fatalities have been directly attributed to this.

I recommend identifying who is specifically responsible for supervising which children and for what time. Do allow time for the person supervising to have a break so they can enjoy themselves too.

Keep a very close eye on sensory seeking children. It is very easy for them to become so focused on their sensory seeking that they become unaware of other sensory inputs, such as a parent calling urgently for the children to exit the water. These children can push themselves despite fatigue, thirst, hunger, injury, or need for the bathroom in such a sensory rich environment. It is necessary to ensure they stop and take care of their other needs. Sensory seeking children are more likely to push boundaries, both yours and their own.

Be very aware of children playing in rock pools and on rocks, even experienced swimmers are washed out to sea in these places.

There have been a number of tragic cases of children digging deep holes and becoming trapped under the sand when the sides collapse in. At all times monitor your children closely even if they are not near the water as the water is not the only danger on a beach.

Sensory sensitive children can find a beach environment extremely overwhelming. The noise of the ocean, other children running around making unexpected noises, screeching seagulls, music players, and the sound sand makes under foot can all be irritating to a child with sound sensitivity.

The sand, seashells, salt water, seaweed, salty air, moisture in the air, sunblock, sunglasses, sun hat, swim suit, and swim shirts can all irritate children with tactile sensitivity.

To help reduce this I recommend trialling the following and find which strategies help your child:

- providing a sun shelter or tent;
- picnic seat;
- blanket or blow up swimming pool and tools for sand play;
- stinger suit (long sleeved, long pants swimming suit),
- wetsuit boots or other beach shoes;
- noise reducing headphones;
- sunglasses;
- sun hat;
- scent free or hypoallergenic sunscreen.

To help reduce sensory overload, allow your child to choose to what extent they touch tactile inputs. Allow them to have control and choices, such as offering a choice of sand toys rather than forcing contact with tactile inputs that your child finds irritating. Taking a blow up swimming pool so they can cool off in the water safely or simply play without having to touch the sand can help for tactile sensitive children.

For a child that is tactile sensitive or prone to sensory overload, a thin wet suit, especially if it is half a size to one size too small, can provide overall proprioceptive input to the body. It also reduces contact with sand and provides some sun protection. Be aware of overheating as neoprene can trap heat.

Chapter 31: Visiting Relatives

Depending on your family, your extended family may be people that you are related to but you may be practically strangers to each other.

If your family has not yet come to an understanding of what your child's abilities are or how their needs differ, you can try providing information booklets. Make a story book for them (which you can also use with your children) explaining what your child likes and doesn't like.

You can try to talk to them in advance and explain your needs; such as needing to have cupboard locks on the kitchen, plans to reduce escapism, or special dietary needs.

You can invite them to join online social groups that you have found to be helpful.

If your family are not willing to make changes to accommodate your child's special needs consider modifying your plans. Find local accommodation and visit for the day, returning to your alternative accommodation when needed. For example, if your child can no longer cope with the noise or crowds you have a safe, quiet place to go and rest.

Even with an accommodating extended family it is unlikely that you will be able to make their home as safe for your child as your own home is.

Consider the following:

- Can you take along kitchen cupboard/oven locks to increase safety?
- Can you take your outlet covers if you are using them at home?

Create a safe room for your child where you can all relax; have their preferred toys and tools, have somewhere for them to jump and climb without having to worry about breaking family heirlooms.

Is there an area where your child can play and you can relax? Or will you be required to be on alert the entire time? You need to be able to relax too. Can you negotiate to create a safe area for your child to play? Can you negotiate with your relatives for a family member to take time to play with your child and watch over them so you can enjoy your vacation too?

When visiting my family in Australia for over one month, I was able to create a safe room for ourselves where every evening we retreated for some calm time away from the family. Somewhere my son could jump, climb, and play without constantly hearing "no", "NO", "no", because they had been unable to make changes to create a child safe environment. I could see by the end of the day my son was exhausted by the constant demands to comply with their rules and needed to relax where he could freely play.

If you are staying with relatives consider planning some day activities for yourselves which your children will enjoy that don't involve your relatives.

- Play outdoors;
- Do outdoor chores – for example working in the garden, children often love to do gardening and it provides rich sensory experiences;
- Walk to your local park – there are lots of opportunities to do heavy work, and actively engage in proprioceptive play at the park;
- Walk to the local shops and run errands. This is a great way to get some heavy work for your children by allowing them to carry bags (remember no more than 10 percent of your child's body weight). Let

them stop if they report discomfort or appear to be fatigued.

Your family will most likely appreciate help with chores and it can give you some time alone with your child.

Completing chores in the house or garden provides excellent learning opportunities for children and gives good sensory inputs.

Think about how much proprioceptive input you receive from:

- Laundry – pulling heavy, wet clothes or towels from a washing machine;
- Hanging laundry – good proprioception from carrying the basket, stretching, and lifting the clothes to be hung;
- Squeezing pegs;
- Mopping – carrying a bucket of water and using a mop – heavy lifting, pushing and pulling;
- Scrubbing – good proprioception from pushing and pulling movement against a surface;
- Watering plants – good proprioception from carrying and tipping a bucket or watering can.

Family more than anyone else, will provide you with unsolicited advice. I recommend you just act gracefully and thank them for their care. If you practise what you can say in advance, practise self-calming techniques, and preplan plenty of time-outs for yourself it can be helpful. Avoid losing your temper; you have to see your family again.

If your child has special dietary needs here are a few tips that you might consider:

- Offer to prepare the family's food so everyone eats the special diet;

- Feed your child well at meals to reduce the number of snacks needed;
- Provide hearty snacks if you know they will not eat well at main meals with the family, and you can know they have had sufficient intake;
- Make sure you are the one serving your child's meals as family members may be tempted to add a spoonful of that dish that you "just have to try";
- Seat your child beside or even between parents or older siblings;
- If you are going to a potluck, ensure you take along a few choices that meet your child's dietary needs.

You may want to take along your child's favourite plate, bowl, cup, or cutlery if they have inflexibility or sensory issues. If cooking for your child is going to be difficult at your relative's home, consider preparing cooked meals in advance and freeze them, so they can be available as you need them.

Managing special occasions can be especially difficult. Music, crowds of people, and loud unexpected noises (such as Christmas crackers, fireworks, and toys) are often involved.

To prepare your child for events ensure you have your sensory tool kit. Provide your children with choices to give them some control over their environment. Let them know what to expect – can you watch videos or look at photos of previous family get togethers?

During events give your child breaks from having to meet your demands or "perform" for relatives. You might have to take them for a walk in a pram, drive around the block, play outside, read a quiet story, play on a tablet, or other preferred activity.

If you are expecting there to be a crowd of people, arriving early to allow your child to adapt to the environment can be helpful. As people slowly arrive your child can habituate over time to the increasing sensory demands. This also means if you need to leave early it won't be causing as much fuss as you have already been there and had a chance to mingle with everyone.

Identify a quiet area your child can go to if they become overwhelmed.

Where possible allow your child to play in a secure garden. Outside will most likely be quieter and your child can have the chance to engage in heavy work in their play which will help regulate their sensory system. Climbing, jumping, and lugging heavy objects are all calming to the nervous system.

Manage your own expectations; of course, this is very hard. We all want to have peaceful, joyful family events. This just isn't realistic for most of us. For whatever reason when children are involved there is always going to be something going on.

Expect things will go wrong. Rehearse in advance what you will say and do in likely scenarios. Be prepared then make the choice to relax and choose not to take offence at comments made.

Child proof as much as possible and be prepared to replace damaged items if necessary.

Despite our best efforts and being on high alert, during our last family visit our 2-year-old broke an antique window with a toy bat, costing hundreds of dollars to replace; he lost a set of keys; damaged a TV screen; and drew on an antique couch with a pen.

Choose to laugh when things go wrong or at least maintain an "oh, well" attitude. Your mood and tone can help set the mood and tone of the family.

Take along at least more than one pair of spare clothes even if it is just for a day visit. You can be sure that at the very least food will be spilt.

Even for children who are toilet trained If you have difficult relatives who are unaccepting of the realities of life with young children the stress, new environment or change in routine can cause toileting accidents. Take along nappies as a back up during naptime or take along a waterproof bed sheet.

You know your family, if you anticipate that staying with them for an extended time period will be challenging, plan in advance how you might be able to cope with this. If you know your family are particularly difficult, don't plan to stay with them. Meet them out for lunch or even coffee. Meet at the park or beach so there is an activity to keep everyone busy, particularly if you have an active child.

Meet them for lunch instead of dinner (or vice versa), think about at which meal your child is better able to cope with demands.

Can you have other activities scheduled to give yourselves time out?

Investigate a "Plan B" for your accommodation. Is there a hotel nearby? Or a family friend you can stay with? Perhaps you can tell your family in advance that you are unsure of exactly how long you are able to stay. Then they will not feel uncomfortable if you leave earlier than you had planned.

Having plenty of rewards for your children can be helpful. They are in a new environment, being placed under constant demands, and being able to provide positive reinforcement can be helpful for them. Have little gifts, treats, their favourite music on a portable player, or DVD's on an electronic device.

Chapter 32: Tips for Camping

Camping is such a fun and affordable way to have a family holiday. Take lots of photos so you can use them for future stories. One of the biggest benefits of camping is how it reduces all of the distractions we have in our modern society. Nature sounds and being closer to the earth can be extremely calming for the whole family. As it is the most affordable holiday option, aside from staying with relatives and friends, it is a great way to relax without the cost of the trip playing on the back of your mind. You may find your child responds well to a more natural environment such as camping or even farm stays.

Before you go review your previous holiday stories with your child. Do you have any of your own camping videos? If not, can you find some positive camping videos online?

When booking your site, check if there are cabin options as a backup if your tent experience isn't working out. You may want to ask in advance what the bathrooms are like. What are the showers like?

If you are going for the full outdoor experience you can practise using your portable shower and other devices in advance. Your kids will love setting up camp in the backyard for a night and this is a great way to check that nothing is missing from your tent kits.

What local activities are available that are suitable for children?

Make sure you pack activities such as games that your children can enjoy. Also remember to pack car chargers for electronic equipment and spare batteries for any devices or toys that your child is reliant on.

Check fire restrictions in advance and adhere closely to them. If you are planning a bonfire make sure you leave extra space in the fire pit and sit further back from the fire. You want to increase the distance between your child and the fire to give more time to respond should they unexpectedly approach the fire. A child who has never approached a fire may suddenly and without explanation approach it.

Please be prepared for the unexpected. Fire blankets, water, and even an extinguisher should be available just in case. Take great precaution during cooking as hot surfaces will be easily accessible.

If your child wanders, a GPS tracking device can be an option. Plan carefully where your child will sleep if they are prone to nighttime wandering. You may need to sleep across the entranceway to ensure you are woken if your child attempts to leave the tent while you are sleeping.

If you don't want to sleep in a tent, campsites typically offer options such as cabins, caravans, a room with bunks and a shared communal kitchen. Some sites will have cabins with private bathrooms or communal bathrooms. If your child has special needs or is up to use the bathroom frequently at night, paying a small extra fee to rent a cabin with a private bathroom can make your trip much easier.

If you are going bushwalking (trekking) remember to consider your child's physical endurance. A child that appears to be very energetic and always running may actually have low levels of physical fitness over an extended time period (endurance). They may cope well with spurts of activity but be unable to produce consistent effort over a long period of time.

Take along snacks, chewies, water, and any light, preferred sensory tools that your child is attached to.

Be prepared to turn back. If your child becomes overtired you may end up having to carry them.

Plan your walks ahead of time and check routes to see if your walk takes you past cliff edges or water so that you can take additional precautions. Allocate responsibility for supervising your child specifically to one person if you are participating in group activities. This is so that you can avoid issues if you thought another parent or adult was caring for the child.

Camping has some amazing space saving devices that you can get from your local camping store; you can have a great trip with just the basics:

- Backpacks;
- Camelback water packs are great for providing oral input, keeping hydrated and can be easily carried in your backpack giving some proprioceptive input;
- Food (of course!);
- Games;
- Wet weather gear such as rain coats or waterproof shoes so your activities can continue despite a bit of rain;
- Swimming gear if you are near water;
- Basic camping equipment such as tents and sleeping bags;
- Medical kit;
- Comfortable shoes and clothes;
- Camera and video camera;
- Activity specific equipment (such as enclosed shoes for walking or horse riding);
- Remember to take along your own games and options for wet weather and any electronic devices your child is attached to.

Depending on your location you will be able to enjoy many therapeutic activities, such as swimming, canoeing, kayaking, surfing, horse riding, bushwalking/trekking, climbing, and bike riding. Often campsites have games halls with play equipment like table tennis. Check in advance what is available in the location you are staying at.

If you are concerned about disturbing other campers, if your child is quite noisy (or tantrums loudly), you might wish to choose a cabin instead of staying in a tent. If you are staying in a tent you may wish to carefully choose the location of your tent. Being downwind of other campers will mean any noise is less likely to affect others, and you can pitch your tent further away from others if you prefer.

Remember you have the option of putting your child in the car and going for a short drive if this calms them down. Also the car can be a quiet, safe place for them if you sit with them in the back and help them to calm down if they are distressed or overwhelmed.

If your child has physical limitations I suggest considering staying in a cabin instead of a tent. Some tent styles can accommodate a person with mobility issues, especially the larger tents where you have plenty of space to move around.

Check bathroom facilities in advance, and you can even ask them to send you a photo.

You can plan ahead with your occupational therapist how you can overcome any specific issues in the environment you will be staying in. Such as, transfers from chair to tent beds and back, or how to best utilise existing bathroom facilities based on the information you can access from the campsite.

If your child uses an electric wheelchair consider how it will be charged and bring along a spare battery.

Chapter 33: Theme Parks

Theme parks are so much fun. Kids and adults love them; however when visiting a theme park the entire experience can be extremely overwhelming. Whether it is riding repeatedly around the same ride with its canned music, or the extensive queues in the hot sun; by the end of the day you may well be swearing off ever going on a vacation again. Here are some tips to help reduce the stress of the day.

If you are visiting a theme park in your home country (where you have a driving licence and know the road rules), you may find it convenient to rent a car rather than using a bus or taxi for transport. This gives you the benefit of having a backup for storing extra items. Such as changes of clothes for the family, additional food, spare batteries, and anything else you want to take along but simply cannot justify carrying all day. Additionally, having a car on site gives you a safe quiet space for you and your child to go if they become overwhelmed.

Arriving early to the park will allow you to park closer and the park will be somewhat quieter, meaning you can ride the most popular rides before the queues become more extensive midmorning. You may be eligible to apply for a temporary disability parking permit; you can speak to your paediatrician regarding this as regulations change from time to time.

If your child requires a nap and cannot fit into a stroller or pram, having your car onsite gives you a good option for them to rest while your partner or other carer continue inside the park with your other children.

Having your own car available means you have full control over when you leave the park and are not left having to manage your children on a bus or taxi queue after a full day in a park.

Please note that if you are travelling internationally, driving in a foreign environment can be extremely stressful. Depending on which country you hold your driving license in, you may be required to register for an international drivers license.

Remember to always carry the card for your accommodation, particularly if you do not speak the local language. This will help allow locals to assist you with directions despite potential language barriers.

Packing your own food can save you a lot of money. Most theme parks will inspect bags to prevent you from bringing in outside food or drinks. A brief doctor's letter explaining your child has food sensitivities and requires a special diet can help to ensure you don't over spend on food. It helps keep your child healthy by avoiding the junk food with its sugar highs and subsequent lows. It also helps you to avoid the low fiber, high fat foods with food dyes, preservatives, and additives such as flavor enhancers that you do not usually provide to your child and could result in unexpected reactions.

Carry a light cooler bag with soft sides as this has the advantage of collapsing as you use the contents. Placing ice cubes into zip-lock bags gives you an affordable, disposable ice pack that you can discard as they melt. Place a partially filled water bottle into your freezer on its side and top up with water when you are ready to take it, to give yourself a nice cool supply. Do not expect to be able to find food for restricted diets inside a theme park. Make sure you bring along snacks and meals. You can make sandwiches fun by using cookie cutters to make them interesting, (like a star shaped sandwich). Fruit can be fun too, for example melon balls with different melons being used, or cut into shapes using cookie cutters, even thin slices of apple can be shaped using a metal cookie cutter. Dried fruits can be made into necklaces for a chewy snack; just be sure your child does not eat any string.

If you view the theme park's website in advance you can often print off maps, schedules and watch videos of rides. You may want to check with the park when their off season is, and then you can expect the park to be quieter.

Planning your day ahead of time can make a huge difference to your experience. Highlight bathroom locations. Consider when rides will be more in demand, such as rides for infants generally have more demand in the mornings and become quieter in the late afternoon. Whereas, the more daring rides are often quieter early in the morning and become busier around lunchtime and afternoons into the evenings.

In the late afternoon while at Dream World on the Gold Coast in Australia, my sister ended up riding around a single ride (Wiggles World) fifteen times in total, as we were able to get off the ride, walk around and go straight back on again; whereas in the morning the queue had been more than an hour long. I had the ride's theme song in my head for months after that trip.

If your child has difficulty queuing up, check if the theme park has access cards. Disneyland has recently launched the Disability Access Service card; you can check their website for information on how the program works. They will need to know what specific accommodations your child needs. Many parks have a similar program available.

If you are travelling to Walt Disney World I recommend obtaining an official guide, such as Fodor's Guide. The park is like a small city and you should read the book prior to visiting. You can order maps in advance from the Walt Disney World website, but do order well in advance to allow for shipment times. The park is so large you simply cannot go on every ride. Watch video clips of rides to help your

124

child become familiar with them and to select which you would like to try during your visit.

Some restaurants in Walt Disney World cater to special diets. Research and book your reservations well in advance, giving them your special requirements at the time of reservation.
Keep in mind a theme park trip is an expensive holiday option, even more so for destinations like Walt Disney World. Ensure you have a lot of padding in your planned budget for unexpected expenses in addition to the entrance fees. Such as, snacks and drinks, professional photos from rides and with the parks themed characters, toys, balloons, gifts, park t-shirts, hats, towels, postcards, and other souvenirs, that both adults and kids can end up becoming caught up in.

If the theme park you are visiting does not provide special considerations for children or adults with special needs, you will need to support your child while they are standing in line.

It is important to know your child's sensory needs well in advance so you can plan your trip accordingly.

Touch Sensitivity

If your child is touch sensitive, make sure there is a space around them, use yourself or a pram to reduce incidental touch.

Pressure vests (or compression vests) can be used to help reduce touch sensitivity.

You can provide oral input such as chewy jewellery, chewing gum (if age appropriate), particularly chewing to provide heavy work for the mouth which can help reduce sensitivity.

Massage and tight hugs can help reduce touch sensitivity.

Placing your child in a stroller while standing in line can help them to avoid incidental touch. Though I do recommend you ensure that your child has plenty of time to walk and run around during the day.

If your child is younger they may enjoy being carried in a carrier. Practice in advance both for your child and to increase your endurance for carrying them for longer time periods.

Sensory Avoiding

If your child tends to avoid sensory inputs or becomes easily overwhelmed providing the option of noise reduction headphones, sunglasses, and hats can be helpful to reduce sensory input.

Providing consistent proprioceptive input through pressure vests or backpacks can help reduce sensitivity.

Do not pressure or force your child onto a ride that they do not feel comfortable riding on. Their increased anxiety combined with the rides input can lead to sensory overload.

Low arousal

If your child has low arousal and then goes onto a very stimulating ride it can be a completely unexpected experience. It can cause anxiety or even fear and send your child into sensory overload. While you are queuing up with your child it can be helpful to explain what they will see and experience during the ride. Let them know if there will be flashing lights, spinning, bumps, or splashing water. Ensure your child is aware of what they will experience.

You can also provide organising sensory input which includes proprioception for the body, and oral heavy work such as chewing and sucking.

Sensory Seeking

If your child is a sensory seeker, standing in line can be very difficult. If you can find a way to provide your child with organising sensory input while in the queue it will greatly help your child to remain in their place.

Provide lots of proprioceptive input; give heavy work, or give vestibular input that is calm and consistent (like swinging back and forward instead of spinning on the spot). Allow fun rides and follow up with heavy work and proprioception to reduce becoming overwhelmed. For example, after the ride your child carries the backpack with the drinks.

You can provide oral input including sucking and chewing on toys and foods. Provide fiddle toys; these can be attached to backpacks by a short cord, which will help to ensure they are not lost.

You can encourage on the spot exercises and games such as, Simon Says, I Spy, push pull games with parents, or "thumb wars" games. Before and after rides encourage your child to press their hands together in prayer pose and be strong, then hook fingertips together and pull strongly.

Provide music to listen to that your child enjoys. Give simple responsibilities such as carrying a pack.

Reducing the risk of sensory overload on theme park rides.

Talk to your child about the ride they will be going on. You can say things such as: "We leave our bags in a set place" (especially if your child is attached to particular items); "the ride is going to be fun, the music is loud, the lights will be flashing"; "it is exciting"; "I will be sitting beside you".

If it is a water ride talk to your child about the noise of the water, the seat being wet, and getting splashed by the water.

Anticipation of the incoming sensory input helps your child to categorise the sudden rush of information. The sensations you feel on many theme park rides are extremely threatening without the context of the park and all the safety measures you know are in place. However, even the rides designed for children involve bumping and spinning, and can be unpredictable, particularly when you include the other children and their responses of giggling, screaming, and laughing. These responses might be completely unexpected for your child. You can provide them the context for what is going on and this will help reduce your child's anxiety.

Anxiety will greatly contribute to sensory overload. If a child is anxious they will cognitively interpret incoming sensory information within that context. This can cause a child to become overwhelmed quicker and easier than usual.

Do not pressure your child to go on a ride even if you have queued up for it, as this will increase their anxiety and can lead to sensory overload. Never force your child to go onto a ride they are uncomfortable with, as this will most likely result in a sensory-based meltdown or an anxiety driven behavioural outburst.

Provide context for your child by explaining what is happening and how long it will last. Ensure you are nearby as you can act as a safe base for your child.

Providing noise cancelling headphones and sound therapy music can help if your child has noise sensitivity.

Proprioception is one of the most effective ways to calm the central nervous system. Active participation is more effective, meaning giving your child an active role, such as completing heavy work tasks, will be more effective than having them passively sit while you give them proprioception through massage or weight. Active proprioception can be gained by carrying packs, pushing the pram, push-pull games, chewing or blowing resistance toys, and opening containers like zip-lock bags, lunchboxes, or twist top containers which are more difficult for children.

Remember all children, and even adults, will become tired and irritable from a long, full day out and will need time to rest. Sitting and watching shows can be beneficial to give everyone in your family a break from walking and queues.

Meltdowns

If your child has a sensory meltdown or is engaging in undesirable behaviours there are a number of things you can do.

The main thing is to remove the sensory input that is causing your child to be overwhelmed. Noise, visual input, and vestibular input can all contribute to becoming overwhelmed.

Before you enter the park and start to enjoy your day take the time to identify quieter areas of the park and bathrooms so that you can easily locate them.

An oversized stroller with a blanket can be used to create a secure "quiet space" away from incidental touch and visual inputs.

You can provide proprioception with a long firm hug, massage, a compression vest, or backpack with some weight (no more than 10 percent of your child's body weight).

If your child has not yet reached the point of meltdown but is becoming overwhelmed you can take them to a quiet place and provide sensory tools based on what you know your child prefers. Provide your child's favourite toy if you know this is calming for them. An iPad or device with your child's favourite program or favourite music could also help your child to relax.

Waterparks

Being in a swimming pool is generally considered to be calming; in contrast water parks are loud with unpredictable noises, water currents, and splashes. Children can become quickly overwhelmed in this environment. Additionally after swimming children are often more hungry and more tired than you would expect compared to the same time playing on the land.

Be sure you provide plenty of drinking water, sunblock, sun shirts, hats, and sunglasses. Sensory avoiders may prefer to wear a stinger suit (or a light neoprene wet suit). In this environment you must watch sensory seeking children extremely closely. It is very easy for children to move between areas and they need to remain in sections where their swimming skills are sufficient.

In water play environments it is very easy for your child to get sunstroke, sun burnt, or even hypothermia. This can happen without them being aware of it because children get so caught up in their play. Watch for the signs of these in your child.

Ensure you are extremely clear about which adult is watching which child. It is so easy to think another person is monitoring the children, even more so when you are with a group of adults. Specifically allocating who is monitoring who and for how long can greatly reduce the risk that no one is directly supervising the children despite there being multiple adults. Again, please teach your children to swim and ensure the adults in your family complete a CPR course.

Chapter 34: Shopping Trip Tips

Since so many holidays require shopping trips in the preparation phase, and often include recreational shopping trips at malls, street markets, and bazaars I have included some tips for shopping with your child.

Sound sensitivity – Provide noise reducing headphones. If you feel these are too noticeable you can experiment with swimmers earplugs or waxes that can be shaped to the ear. Please follow manufacturer's instructions, particularly safety precautions, and do not use if your child is still swallowing small parts or mouthing small objects.

Providing your child's favorite music or sound therapy music on a portable player can be calming for your child.

Light sensitivity – Allow your child to wear sunglasses or a hat to reduce their exposure to the store lights. The fluorescent lights can be difficult to cope with for some children.

Tactile sensitivity – If you are buying clothes, trying on one item and then using that as a basis for selecting other pieces can help reduce the number of times your child has to try on clothing. Ensure you avoid rough seams, zippers directly on the skin (as you see in some shirt styles), and rough fabrics particularly some acrylics. Look for brushed cotton. There are companies that now provide clothing especially for children with tactile sensitivity. Seamless underpants and socks are available.

Ensure you can remove tags. Be thoughtful about the styling around the neck. If your child is sensitive they may be unable to tolerate fabric close to their neck and may prefer V-neck or otherwise open neck styles.

Escapism – If your child is known to escape consider if you can use a large pram for them for the duration of the shopping trip. If your child will wear a backpack, you can attach a strap from the bag to yourself rather than attaching directly to your child. There are products available for young children with this built into the design. We received a lovely monkey with a strap attached instead of the monkey tail, which allows the parent to have a backup in case the child drops their parent's hand.

Tantrum – If your child frequently tantrums in public determine if it is a behavioural issue, and hence a tantrum, or if it is a sensory-based meltdown. If it is a sensory-based meltdown determine what could be contributing and address the factors one by one.

Behaviour has a purpose; it is typically either seeking attention or to get away from something (including to get out of doing something). To manage tantrums start with short trips and build up to longer trips as you see success in managing your child's behaviours. Be very consistent in how you respond to their behaviour. Provide positive reinforcement (rewards) for correct behaviour and ignore the behaviours you do not want.

Never threaten your child with abandonment. Do not offer rewards or threaten punishments that you cannot implement. This teaches your child to ignore you.

As a clinician and parent I have heard hundreds of parents talking to their children. I have seen that often we as adults can get caught up in how busy we are and forget how we are speaking to our children.

I can clearly recall one instance when the child had refused to put on their shoes after having a session with a therapist. Parents who state they will not take a child home until they put on their shoes are setting themselves up for more challenging behaviour. Can you honestly sit there for 3 to 4 hours while you wait out your child's stubborn behaviour? What most likely will occur is what happened in the instance

I observed – the parent switched to offering a reward. "Put on your shoes and I will give you a lolly". It didn't work. The parent was then scrambling for another threat or reward, each time the reward and threat escalated and no action was being taken.

A sensible solution to this issue is "Put your shoes on" … child refuses. "Okay we have to go. The ground is hard and your feet will hurt. Put your shoes on". Child refuses. "Okay, we are going now." Barefoot child starts to walk on the hot, rough, or stony ground and responds to the environmental input. Adult responds, "Oh the ground is hurting your feet. That's why we need our shoes. Put your shoes on" … the child will in all likelihood comply and put on their shoes (simplify the language based on your child's abilities).

In this instance you have not given your authority away as the adult, you have allowed a natural consequence. This will reinforce your authority as the caring adult and increases the chance next time you make a request that your child will comply because they learn to understand your requests are there for their benefit. Of course you must ensure that no actual harm comes to your child. Natural consequences must not be harmful and should be appropriate for your child's age and ability levels.

Chapter 35: Building Your Sensory Tool Kit

Occupational Therapists frequently prescribe "sensory diets" to clients giving families sensory based activities to incorporate throughout their day however the most recent thinking in the area of sensory processing supports the concept of a "sensory toolkit". Where a range of appropriate activities, equipment and strategies are recommended to the family based on the child's sensory needs and families learn how to select appropriate strategies to use before and after challenging sensory experiences. This empowers families and children to manage their sensory processing needs in a flexible, real life way.

If your child has a sensory processing disorder an occupational therapist can help identify challenging areas, environmental triggers and help families to determine which are the most effective strategies and tools for your child.

I am including some tips, which you can try with your child however if your child has sensory processing difficulties, many of which can be hidden and difficult to determine, I do recommend you seek advice from your occupational therapist to develop the most effective tool kit for your child.

Having a sensory toolkit with you during your travels will help your child cope during transit times and will be helpful if you find yourself inside with nothing to do which can happen due to weather or plans falling through.

For any issues you are facing there are two options, modify the environment or help your child to modify their response to the environmental stimuli.

Tools for your tool kit

Please adapt your tool kit contents to meet the needs of your child and their personal preferences. Do discuss with your occupational therapist if you are unsure about the effectiveness or use of any items mentioned.

Oral Motor Tools

- Chewable jewelry – chewing - building oral motor strength

- Chewies – chewing - building oral motor strength

- Resistance whistles – blowing - building oral motor strength, increasing breath control, improving lip closure

- Curly straws – sucking – building oral motor strength, increasing oral motor control, sucking thick fluids improves strength, using straws can improve lip closure.

- Chewy foods – such as dried fruits, dehydrated vegetables, when age and developmentally appropriate can provide chewing gum - provides interesting textures, chewing can be calming.

- Crunchy foods – such as fresh apples, very dry fruits and vegetables – provides interesting textures as part of a range of rich sensory experiences and can be calming for some children.

Proprioception Tools

- Compression vests – worn on the body – provide consistent moderate pressure onto the body helping to reduce sensitivity, calming.

- Weighted equipment including backpacks, weighted vests, weighted toys, weighted blankets – worn on the body – use with extreme caution and only under constant competent adult supervision, no more than 10% of the child's body weight should be applied. Use for a limited time period, 10 minutes per hour is a good reference point.

- Wrestling games such as thumb wars, tug of war, play wrestling with a parent – no specialised equipment required.

- Theraputty™, stress balls, soft toys - something to squeeze.

- Therabands™, stretchy toys - something to pull.

- Lifting a small bucket of water or sand (a general guide for children is to lift no more than 10% of their body weight).

- Digging in the sand or a garden.

- Climbing such as climbing a rope ladder, hanging bars, climbing frames, rock climbing – vestibular and proprioceptive input is gained from these activities.

Intense proprioceptive input is gained at the joints and muscles during climbing and hanging from the hands activities and these can be very beneficial for developing body awareness, coordination, building self-confidence when completed under competent adult supervision using safe equipment.

Auditory Tools

- Sound therapy programs – prescribed by therapists – special equipment required. Can be very helpful for reducing sound sensitivities and increasing attention in some individuals.

- Noise reduction headphones – easily applied in a noisy environment.

- Swimming ear plugs or ear waxes – particularly if your child is sensitive to water being in their ears. Note due to the size parents will need to monitor to ensure they are not chewed or swallowed.

- White noise machines or background music such as wave or nature CDs –effectiveness varies based on the individual experiment to determine your child's preferences.

- Audio players – Mp3s, iPads ™, iPods ™, Leap Pads™ can provide hours of entertainment. Music has be shown repeatedly to improve mood and has even been linked with other benefits such as increased attention, improved learning and even better pain tolerance in some studies.

Tactile play

Fun and a rich sensory experience messy play is an important part of childhood development. Of course provide competent adult supervision for all activities.

- Shaving foam
- Toothpaste

- Paint
- Play dough
- Bubble solutions
- Bath crayons
- Shredded paper
- Glue
- Sticker play
- Rice, legume, pasta, bean or sand trays with toys to bury, shovels and other tools to explore with.
- Scrap fabrics of different textures can be made into toys, blankets, tunnels, tug of war 'ropes'.
- Feeding themselves finger foods
- Cooking – stirring food in the bowl, kneading, using rolling pins, putting mixtures into cooking trays and other safe steps - do not allow access to dangerous objects such as heat surfaces, hot water, knives or any other dangers in your kitchen. Provide competent adult supervision.

Visual Tools

These can be great fun for children particularly when in the car or in any area where space is limited and you don't want a lot of noise. These toys are affordable and can be easily found on online stores such as Amazon. They make excellent surprise presents or "lucky dips" for car rides.

- Flashing balls
- Glow sticks
- Glow in the dark stickers
- Liquid motion toys (can be sand or oil based) provide a nice calming visual.
- Water and glitter filled wands provide a nice calming visual
- Flashing LED or glowing toys.
- Fiber optic lights

Fiddle toys

These toys are affordable and can be easily found on online stores such as Amazon. They make excellent surprise presents or "lucky dips" for car rides, bus, train and plane trips.

- Stretchy toys, such as stretchy frogs, stretchy strings, balls, putty, inside out balls.
- Play dough
- Sticky toys
- Tangles
- Fidget spinners

For children who do not mouth objects and are developmentally able to complete the project without chewing or swallowing small parts make your own jewelry sets can be fun.

Building toys such as Lego™, Mr. Potato Head™ - please only use when developmentally appropriate due to the risk of chewing or swallowing small parts.

To all the families who have read this far:

I wish you happy travels both home and abroad as you travel through this sensory world.